Planning and Assessment in Higher Education

Planning and Assessment in Higher Education

Demonstrating Institutional Effectiveness

Michael F. Middaugh

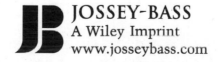

JOSSEY-BASS
A Wiley Imprint
www.josseybass.com

Published by Jossey-Bass
A Wiley Imprint
989 Market Street, San Francisco, CA 94103-1741—www.josseybass.com

Jossey-Bass books and products are available through most bookstores. To contact Jossey-Bass directly call our Customer Care Department within the U.S. at 800-956-7739, outside the U.S. at 317-572-3986, or fax 317-572-4002.

Jossey-Bass also publishes its books in a variety of electronic formats. Some content that appears in print may not be available in electronic books.

Library of Congress Cataloging-in-Publication Data

Middaugh, Michael F., 1945-
   Planning and assessment in higher education : demonstrating institutional effectiveness / Michael F. Middaugh.—1st ed.
      p. cm.—(The Jossey-Bass higher and adult education series)
   Includes bibliographical references and index.
   ISBN 978-0-470-40090-6
   1.   Education, Higher—Planning. 2. Universities and colleges—Administration. 3. Education, Higher—Standards. 4. Education, Higher—Economic aspects 5. Educational evaluation.
   6. Educational accountability.   I. Title.
   LB2341.M4437 2010
   378.1'07—dc22   2009025592

Printed in the United States of America

First Edition

HB Printing 10 9 8 7 6 5 4 3 2

The Jossey-Bass
Higher and Adult Education Series

Contents

Preface

This book is the culmination of experiences acquired during over twenty-five years in the field of institutional research and, most recently, seven years as a commissioner with the Middle States Commission on Higher Education, one of six regional higher education accrediting bodies in the United States. During my quarter century in institutional research, I have had the good fortune to work for three institutions whose senior leadership valued institutional assessment as a tool for informing strategic planning. This was nowhere more true than at the University of Delaware, where I was given broad latitude in shaping analytical strategies to support a broad range of academic, student support, and budget planning activities. Because of my familiarity with the University of Delaware, especially the strategic planning challenges that it faced in the early 1990s, it offers a particularly rich example for illustrating the linkages between assessing and developing measures of institutional effectiveness and using that assessment information as the basis for strategic institutional decisions, especially with respect to allocation of human and fiscal resources. Consequently, I cite that institution throughout this book in illustrating principles related to assessing institutional effectiveness. That said, while the University of Delaware may be a primary illustrative venue, the underlying principles related to assessment are broadly portable across institutional boundaries to other colleges and universities, two-year and four-year alike. Examples from other institutions of this portability are also evident throughout the volume.

Over the past decade, assessment of institutional effectiveness has become a cornerstone for accrediting higher education institutions in the United States. External pressures—particularly from Congress, state legislatures, and parents, especially about escalating tuition rates—are forcing institutions to operate more transparently. That transparency is expected to focus on institutional outcomes, regarding both student learning and the extent to which an institution makes the most effective and efficient use of its human and fiscal resources in support of the teaching/learning process. Those external pressures and the full range of expected outcomes are documented in this volume.

Over the course of my career, higher education has witnessed a host of management strategies, each purporting to be the penultimate solution to our problems, only to be replaced by the next strategy du jour—zero-based budgeting (ZBB), total quality management (TQM), continuous quality improvement (CQI), and the list goes on. There are some who believe that the assessment movement will fall into that category. I do not share that belief. In my view, assessment has become an essential tool for demonstrating the ongoing effectiveness of colleges and universities to those public and private sources that fund us. But more important, assessment has become the primary tool for understanding and improving the ways in which students learn and for developing and enhancing those institutional structures and programs that support student learning. Accreditation agencies—both at the institutional and the programmatic level—are now operating in a "culture of evidence" that requires institutions to qualitatively and quantitatively demonstrate that they are meeting student learning goals and effectively marshalling human and fiscal resources toward that end. And within that culture of evidence, institutions are explicitly required to demonstrate the use of systematic strategic planning, informed by a comprehensive program of assessment, to support teaching and learning. Because accreditation is a prerequisite to institutions receiving Title IV federal student aid, this culture of evidence is not likely to disappear anytime soon.

But rather than view assessment as an external requirement imposed by an accreditor or other entity, institutions should embrace the opportunity to measure student learning and institutional effectiveness as a vehicle for more effectively communicating how they are meeting their respective missions, to both internal and external constituencies. This book will focus on assessment as a language for describing institutional effectiveness, demonstrating that institutional planning is rooted in comprehensive and systematic information, and describing the outcomes of that planning activity.

Successful colleges and universities in the twenty-first century will be characterized by effective assessment and planning. This book is intended to contribute to and to celebrate that outcome. I have a young granddaughter, Jasmine, who is the light of my life and who will all too soon be of college age. I want her to attend an institution that demonstrably focuses on her learning and uses its resources to enhance student success. I hope that this book will contribute in some measure to creating such an environment for her.

Acknowledgments

The development of this book has been influenced by a number of individuals. First and foremost, I would like to acknowledge my friend and colleague, David Hollowell, to whom I reported for over twenty years at the University of Delaware in his capacity as executive vice president and treasurer. David gave me the support and encouragement to be creative in assessments of institutional effectiveness. The Delaware Study of Instructional Costs and Productivity, which is described in this book, could never have become a reality were it not for David's emphasis on the importance of benchmarking information as a tool in effective strategic planning. I would also like to thank David Roselle, former president of the University of Delaware, and Daniel Rich, the former provost at Delaware, for their emphasis on the importance of assessment data in the planning process. And that emphasis is being continued under the stewardship of the current institutional leadership, President Patrick Harker, Executive Vice President and Treasurer Scott Douglass, and Provost Thomas Apple.

Two other individuals have played important roles in shaping my thinking with respect to planning and assessment. I first got to know Peter Burnham, president of Brookdale Community College in New Jersey, when I served on a task force that he was chairing in 2000 to revise the Middle States Commission on Higher Education accreditation standards. For the past three years, he has served as chair of that commission and I as his vice chair. His passion and commitment to the inextricable link between high-quality assessment and excellence in planning have been a source of inspiration. And I would be remiss if I did not acknowledge the work of my longtime friend and colleague, Jeffrey Seybert, director of Institutional Research and Planning at Johnson County Community College in Kansas. Jeff has long been at the forefront of assessment of student learning outcomes, and much of the discussion in this book has been shaped by numerous conversations with him.

Finally, I would like to acknowledge the most important person in my life, my wife, Margaret, who has lovingly supported and encouraged me in my professional endeavors over the years. As some form of retirement is not too far in the offing, I look forward to spending more time with her.

Michael F. Middaugh
Wilmington, Delaware
November 2009

About the Author

Michael F. Middaugh is associate provost for institutional effectiveness at the University of Delaware. In that capacity, he directs all analytical activity directed at assessing institutional effectiveness at the University. He has been at the University for over twenty years, with prior experience on two campuses of the State University of New York. For the past fifteen years he has directed the Delaware Study of Instructional Costs and Productivity, a national data-sharing consortium of over five hundred four-year colleges and universities. Middaugh is a past president of the Society for College and University Planning as well as a past president of the Association for Institutional Research. He is a commissioner and vice chair of the Middle States Commission on Higher Education, one of six regional accrediting agencies in the United States. He is the author of *Understanding Faculty Productivity: Standards and Benchmarks for Colleges and Universities* (Jossey-Bass, 2001), as well as numerous book chapters and articles on instructional costs and faculty productivity.

Middaugh holds a bachelor of science degree in biology from Fordham University, a master of arts in liberal studies degree from the State University of New York at Stony Brook, and a doctor of education degree from the State University of New York at Albany.

Planning and Assessment in Higher Education

1

THE NATIONAL CONTEXT FOR ASSESSMENT

Introduction: The Good Old Days

This book's focus is the inextricable linkage between planning and assessment as characteristics of effective colleges and universities in the twenty-first century. Such a linkage has not always been empha-sized or valued within higher education. During the period from immediately following World War II through the early to mid-1980s, higher education in the United States led what can only be referred to as a charmed existence. Veterans returning from the War flooded into colleges and universities in the late 1940s and early 1950s, and were followed by their offspring—the so-called post-war baby boom—in the 1960s and 1970s. Public college and university enrollments increased exponentially, and so did governmental support. Private colleges and universities shared in the growth as the result of governmentally supported student aid programs. The number of degree programs and disciplines at institutions grew rapidly in response to student demand. This did not require a great deal of careful planning—it was essentially a situation of "build it and they will come." And as long as graduates were produced in those disciplines with knowledge and skills required by business, industry, and government, there were few questions as to how money was being spent. These were halcyon days for higher education.

The environment began to change in the 1980s. The enrollment growth at higher education institutions dwindled as the baby boomers finished cycling through college. Economic recession in the early 1980s forced the federal and state governments to reevaluate their level of support for higher education—and parents to question the tuition levels being charged for their children to attend college. And the priorities for federal and state appropriations began to shift. Underperforming public elementary and secondary schools shifted governmental support for education to the K-12 sector. The erosion of federal and state support for higher education was further exacerbated by rising health care costs requiring greater governmental funding of Medicare and Medicaid and state health plans. Deteriorating highway and bridge infrastructure and demand for additional resources to support public safety issues, most notably construction of new incarceration facilities, further cut into public funds available to higher education. As the 1990s arrived, the financial picture for higher education was becoming increasingly bleak. As public funding declined, tuition levels increased. And as tuition increased, so too did scrutiny of higher education, with serious questions being raised about the quality of the product in which tuition dollars were being invested.

The Gathering Storm

One of the first hints that higher education's free pass to resources was evaporating came with a seminal article in *Change* magazine in 1990, in which Robert Zemsky, from the University of Pennsylvania, and William Massy, of Stanford University, articulated their vision of what they refer to as the "ratchet and lattice" within American colleges and universities:

> [The academic ratchet] is a term to describe the steady, irreversible shift of faculty allegiance away from the goals of a given institution, toward those of an academic specialty. The ratchet denotes the advance of an entrepreneurial spirit among faculty nationwide, leading to increased emphasis on research and publication, and on teaching one's specialty in favor of general introduction courses, often at the expense of coherence in an academic curriculum. Institutions seeking to enhance their own prestige may contribute

to the ratchet by reducing faculty teaching and advising responsibilities across the board, enabling faculty to pursue their individual research and publication with fewer distractions. The academic ratchet raises an institution's costs, and it results in undergraduates paying more to attend institutions in which they receive less attention than in previous decades. (Zemsky and Massy, 1990, 22)

The authors go on to argue that the "academic ratchet," which describes a faculty less concerned with teaching than with other more personally rewarding activities, is invariably accompanied by an "administrative lattice," characterized by burgeoning administrative offices assuming academic functions that were heretofore performed by faculty, such as academic advising, tutoring, and counseling. The administrative lattice further drives up the cost of higher education. Implicit, if not explicit, in the concept of the academic ratchet and administrative lattice in higher education is an enterprise that has lost managerial control over its basic operational functions and is strafed with inefficiencies. In short, the academic ratchet and lattice embody the complete absence of any systematic planning directed at ensuring student learning and enhancing institutional effectiveness. Thus were sown the seeds of discontent that would lead to an outcry in coming years over geometrically escalating tuition costs without an obvious significant return on investment.

In the same year that Zemsky and Massy published their *Change* magazine article, Ernest Boyer published his *Scholarship Reconsidered: Priorities of the Professoriate*, in which he described the changes in American colleges and universities following World War II:

But even as the mission of American higher education was changing, the standards used to measure academic prestige continued to be narrowed. Increasingly, professors were expected to conduct research and publish results. Promotion and tenure depended on such activity, and young professors seeking security and status found it more rewarding—in a quite literal sense—to deliver a paper in New

York or Chicago than teach undergraduates back home. Lip service still was being paid to maintaining a balance between *collegiate* responsibilities and *university* work, but on most campuses the latter had clearly won the day. (Boyer, 1990, 12)

Boyer goes on to say:

Thus, in just a few decades, priorities in American higher education were significantly realigned. The emphasis on undergraduate education, which throughout the years had drawn its inspiration from the colonial college tradition, was being overshadowed by the European university tradition, with its emphasis on graduate education and research. Specifically, at many of the nation's four-year institutions, the focus had moved from the student to the professoriate, from general to specialized education, and from loyalty to the campus to loyalty to the profession. (12–13)

Boyer was strongly arguing that basic general education was being neglected in favor of niche specialties that coincide with faculty research interests. It was becoming increasingly difficult for undergraduates to engage in meaningful ways with tenured and tenure-eligible faculty, in whom the institution has the greatest investment. As the result of these criticisms of higher education, the Carnegie Foundation for the Advancement of Teaching created a National Commission on Educating Undergraduates in 1995. It was initially chaired by Boyer and was subsequently renamed the Boyer Commission following his death. In 1998, the Boyer Commission issued an eagerly anticipated report, titled *Reinventing Undergraduate Education*, which leveled some of the harshest criticism yet on the quality of American postsecondary education. Consider the following assessment of research universities:

To an overwhelming degree, they [research universities] have furnished the cultural, intellectual, economic, and political leadership of the nation. Nevertheless, the research universities have too often

failed, and continue to fail, their undergraduate populations . . .
Again and again, universities are guilty of advertising practices they
would condemn in the commercial world. Recruitment materials
display proudly the world-famous professors, the splendid facilities
and ground breaking research that goes on within them, but
thousands of students graduate without ever seeing the world-
famous professors or tasting genuine research. Some of their instructors are likely to be badly trained or untrained teaching assistants
who are groping their way toward a teaching technique; some others
may be tenured drones who deliver set lectures from yellowed notes,
making no effort to engage the bored minds of the students in front
of them. (Boyer Commission, 1998, 5-6)

While indicting research universities for failing to effectively
manage their most important human resources—faculty—the Boyer
Commission also had much to say about the state of student
learning in higher education:

Many students graduate having accumulated whatever number of
courses is required, but still lacking a coherent body of knowledge, or
any inkling as to how one sort of information might relate to others.
And all too often they graduate without knowing how to think
logically, write clearly, or speak coherently. The university has given
them too little that will be of real value beyond a credential that will
help them get their first jobs. And with larger and larger numbers of
peers holding the same papers in their hands, even that credential
has lost much of its potency. (Boyer Commission, 6)

It was inevitable that this internal criticism within higher
education would spill over into popular media. The 1996 issue
of U.S. News and World Report's annual special issue on "America's
Best Colleges" contained the following scathing commentary:

The trouble is that higher education remains a labor-intensive service
industry made up of thousands of stubbornly independent and

mutually jealous units that support expensive and vastly underused facilities. It is a more than $200 billion-a-year economic enterprise—many of whose leaders oddly disdain economic enterprise, and often regard efficiency, productivity, and commercial opportunity with the same hauteur with which Victorian aristocrats viewed those "in trade" . . . The net result is a hideously inefficient system that, for all its tax advantages and public and private subsidies, still extracts a larger share of family income than almost anywhere else on the planet . . . (*U.S. News and World Report*, 1996, 91)

The article goes on to hypothesize about the underlying causes of inefficiencies at colleges and universities:

For their part, most colleges blame spiraling tuition on an assortment of off-campus scapegoats—congressional budget cutters, stingy state legislatures, government regulators, and parents who demand ever more costly student health and recreational services. Rarely mentioned are the on-campus causes of the tuition crisis: declining teaching loads, non-productive research, ballooning financial aid programs, bloated administrative hierarchies, "celebrity" salaries for professional stars, and inflated course offerings. If colleges and universities were rated on their overall financial acumen, most would be lucky to escape with a passing grade. (91–92)

To sum up the critique of higher education to that point: American colleges and universities were depicted as fundamentally mismanaged, economically inefficient institutions charging dramatically escalating tuition rates for an educational product that was not demonstrably worth the price. Sadly, most colleges and universities lacked the quantitative and qualitative analytical evidence of institutional effectiveness that would enable them to blunt this criticism. Accurate or not, these critical perceptions of higher education went largely unchallenged, suggesting that higher education officials had determined that they were beyond accountability and that transparency in institutional operations was for other enterprises.

Enter the Federal Government

By the end of the 1990s, the crescendo of criticism of higher education had achieved a volume that the federal government could no longer ignore. Preparatory to reauthorizing the Higher Education Act in 1998, Congress earlier established a National Commission on the Cost of Higher Education to study, among other things, the underlying causes of spiraling tuition rates, administrative costs, and trends in faculty workload. The Commission's report, approved in 1998, and titled *Straight Talk About College Costs and Prices*, contained the following observation that set the stage for extended debate in the years to come:

> . . . because academic institutions do not account differently for time spent directly in the classroom and time spent on other teaching and research activities, it is almost impossible to explain to the public how individuals employed in higher education use their time. Consequently, the public and public officials find it hard to be confident that academic leaders allocate resources effectively and well. Questions about costs and their allocation to research, service, and teaching are hard to discuss in simple, straightforward ways and the connection between these activities and student learning is difficult to draw. In responding to this growing concern, academic leaders have been hampered by poor information and sometimes inclined to take issue with those who asked for better data. Academic institutions need much better definitions and measures of how faculty members, administrators, and students use their time. (National Commission on the Cost of Higher Education, 1998, 20)

That institutions lacked the basic data to effectively manage their operations is a damning indictment, particularly when viewed by those outside of higher education who are held highly accountable for institutional effectiveness as a precondition for continued infusion of resources. The Commission went on to say:

The skepticism underlying this concern about where higher education places its priorities is a major consequence of higher education's inability to explain its cost and price structure convincingly to the public. Some cost data are unavailable; much of the information that is provided is hard to understand. College finances are far too opaque. Higher education has a major responsibility to make its cost and price structures much more *"transparent"* [author's emphasis], i.e., easily understandable to the public and its representatives. (20)

The aforementioned reference to transparency in higher education operations was the most visible call for accountability to date. The National Commission on the Cost of Higher Education issued a series of recommendations in 1998 that are as relevant today as when they were promulgated, and certainly provide a vibrant context for the main substance of this book:

1. Academic institutions will intensify their efforts to control costs and increase institutional productivity.

2. The academic community will provide the leadership required to develop better consumer information about costs and prices and to improve accountability to the public.

3. Governments will develop new approaches to academic regulation, approaches that emphasize performance instead of compliance, and differentiation in place of standardization.

4. The academic community will develop well-coordinated, efficient accrediting processes that relate institutional productivity to effectiveness in improving student learning. (National Commission on the Cost of Higher Education, 1998, 15–17)

As this book is being written, there has been, at best, patchy progress in implementation of these decade-old recommendations. Progress has been so slow that, in 2006, U.S. Department of Education Secretary Margaret Spellings commissioned a study of higher education, A *Test of Leadership: Charting the Future of U.S.*

Higher Education. The Report of the Secretary's Commission on the Future of Higher Education, commonly abbreviated as the Spellings Commission, stated,

> We believe that improved accountability is vital to ensuring the success of all of the other reforms we propose. Colleges and universities must become more transparent about cost, price, and student success outcomes, and must willingly share this information with students and families. Student achievement, which is inextricably connected to institutional success, must be measured by institutions on a "value-added" basis that takes into account students' academic baseline when assessing their results. This information should be available to students, and reported publicly in aggregate form to provide consumers and policymakers an accessible, understandable way to measure the relative effectiveness of different colleges and universities. (Spellings Commission, 2006, 4)

There are metrics for assessing cost containment and institutional productivity in higher education, but they are not as widely used as they could be. These metrics will be fully discussed in this volume. With respect to transparency in the cost of a college education, the National Center for Education Statistics (NCES) has developed a website, College Navigator (http://nces.ed.gov/collegenavigator/), a search tool that provides consumers with very basic information on tuition, financial aid, and institutional characteristics for all colleges and universities in the United States receiving Pell Grants. The jury is very definitely out on whether the federal and state governments have moved toward regulation that emphasizes performance over compliance and that celebrates the differentiation of institutional missions rather than applying a one-size-fits-all view of higher education institutions. Accrediting bodies have come closest to fully implementing the recommendation, directed at them by the National Commission on the Cost of Higher Education, that they tie institutional productivity to increased student learning, though they have done so in such a subdued and quiet fashion that most constituencies outside of higher education are unaware of that progress.

A brief word on institutional accreditation in the United States: unlike most industrialized countries with a complex higher education system, the United States does not have a centralized Federal Ministry of Education to regulate that higher education system. Rather, since the beginning of the twentieth century that regulatory responsibility has fallen to regional accrediting bodies. These are membership organizations comprising colleges and universities within a given geographic region who voluntarily engage in a process of peer review, wherein evaluation teams of experts from institutions in the region regularly evaluate other member institutions, determining the extent to which they are in compliance with accreditation standards articulated by each of the regional accrediting bodies to ensure academic quality within those member institutions. This process of peer review and self-regulation has long been the envy of other international colleges and universities, which are bound in a maze of governmental regulations that too often are overly prescriptive and have little to do with enhancing student learning and other institutional outcomes.

Each of the six regional accrediting bodies in the United States has its own discrete set of standards against which it evaluates member institutions for accrediting purposes. In ensuring that those member institutions are more accountable and transparent in their operations, each of the accrediting bodies has emphasized, in its standards, the three critical functions that are the focus of this book: assessment of student learning outcomes, assessment of overall institutional effectiveness, and ongoing strategic planning activity that is informed by those assessments. There is a great deal of commonality in intention, if not in exact wording, in the standards across regions. Consider the comparisons in Table 1.1.

The consistent emphasis by accrediting bodies on demonstrable evidence of assessment of student learning and overall institutional effectiveness, and the use of those assessments in institutional strategic planning, is quite important. All institutions receiving

Table 1-1 Commonality of Standards Across Regional Accrediting Agencies in the United States.

Assessment of Student Learning	Assessment of Institutional Effectiveness	Systematic Strategic Planning
Middle States Association of Colleges and Schools Commission on Higher Education		
Assessment of student learning demonstrates that an institution's students have knowledge, skills, and competencies consistent with institutional goals, and that students at graduation have achieved appropriate higher education goals.	The institution has developed and implemented an assessment process that evaluates its overall effectiveness in achieving its mission and goals, and its compliance with accreditation standards.	An institution conducts ongoing planning and resource allocation based on its mission and goals, develops objectives to achieve them, and utilizes the results of its assessment activities for institutional renewal. Implementation and subsequent evaluation of the success of the strategic plan and resource allocation support the development and change necessary to improve and maintain institutional quality.
New England Association of Colleges and Schools Commission on Institutions of Higher Education		
The institution implements and supports a systematic and broad-based approach to the assessment of student learning focused on educational improvement through understanding what and how students are learning through their academic program and, as appropriate	The institution regularly and systematically evaluates the achievement of its mission and goals, giving primary focus to the realization of its educational objectives. Its system of evaluation is designed to provide relevant and trustworthy information to support institutional	The institution undertakes planning and evaluation appropriate to its needs to accomplish and improve achievement of its mission and purposes. . . . The institution allocates sufficient resources for its planning and evaluation efforts . . . The institution

(continued)

Table 1-1 (Continued)

Assessment of Student Learning	Assessment of Institutional Effectiveness	Systematic Strategic Planning
through experiences outside the classroom.	improvement, with an emphasis on the academic program.	systematically collects and uses data necessary to support its planning efforts and to enhance institutional effectiveness.

North Central Association of Colleges and Schools Higher Learning Commission

Assessment of Student Learning	Assessment of Institutional Effectiveness	Systematic Strategic Planning
The organization provides evidence of student learning and teaching effectiveness that demonstrates it is fulfilling its educational mission.	The organization's ongoing evaluation and assessment processes provide reliable evidence of institutional effectiveness that clearly informs strategies for continuous improvement.	The organization's allocation of resources and its processes for evaluation and planning demonstrate its capacity to fulfill its mission, improve the quality of education, and respond to future challenges and opportunities.

Northwest Commission on Colleges and Universities

Assessment of Student Learning	Assessment of Institutional Effectiveness	Systematic Strategic Planning
The institution offers collegiate level programs that culminate in identified student competencies and lead to degrees or certificates in recognized fields of study. The achievement and maintenance of high quality programs is the primary responsibility of an accredited institution; hence the evaluation of educational programs and their continuous improvement is an ongoing responsibility.	The institution uses the results of its systematic evaluation activities and ongoing planning processes to influence resource allocation and to improve its instructional programs, institutional services, and activities . . . The institution uses information from its planning and evaluation processes to communicate evidence of institutional effectiveness to its public.	The institution engages in ongoing planning to achieve its mission and goals. It also evaluates how well, and in what ways, it is accomplishing its mission and goals, and uses the results for broad-based, continuous planning and evaluation. Through its planning process, the institution asks questions, seeks answers, analyzes itself, and revises its goals, policies, procedures, and resource allocation.

Southern Association of Colleges and Schools Commission on Colleges

The institution identifies college-level general education competencies and the extent to which graduates have attained them.

The institution identifies expected outcomes, and assesses the extent to which it achieves these outcomes, and provides evidence of improvement based on analysis of the results in each of the following areas: educational programs, to include student learning outcomes; administrative support services; educational support services; research within its educational mission, if appropriate; community/public service within its educational mission, if appropriate.

The institution engages in ongoing, integrated, and institution-wide research-based planning and evaluation processes that (1) incorporate a systematic review of institutional mission, goals, and outcomes; (2) result in continuing improvement in institutional quality; and (3) demonstrate the institution is effectively accomplishing its mission.

Western Association of Colleges and Schools Accrediting Commission of Senior Colleges and Universities

The institution's student learning outcomes and expectations for student attainment are clearly stated at the course, program, and as appropriate, institutional level. These outcomes and expectations are reflected in academic programs and policies; curriculum; advisement; library and information resources; and the wider learning

The institution employs a deliberate set of quality assurance processes at each level of institutional functioning, including new curriculum and program approval processes, periodic program review, ongoing evaluation, and data collection. These processes include assessing effectiveness, tracking results over time, using comparative data from

The institution periodically engages its multiple constituencies, including faculty, in institutional reflection and planning processes which assess its strategic position; articulate priorities; examine the alignment of its purposes, core functions and resources; and define the future direction of the

(continued)

Table 1-1 (Continued)

Assessment of Student Learning	Assessment of Institutional Effectiveness	Systematic Strategic Planning
environment . . . The institution demonstrates that its graduates consistently achieve its stated levels of attainment and ensures that its expectations for student learning are embedded in the standards faculty use to evaluate student work.	external sources, and improving structures, processes, curricula, and pedagogy.	institution. The Institution monitors the effectiveness of its plans and planning processes, and revises them as appropriate.

Sources: Middle States Commission on Higher Education, 2006; New England Commission on Institutions of Higher Education, 2005; North Central Higher Learning Commission, 2007; Northwest Commission on Colleges and Universities, 2003; Southern Commission on Colleges, 2007; Western Association of Colleges and Schools, 2001.

federal Title IV financial aid—that is, Pell Grants—must be accredited by a governmentally approved accrediting body. In the vast
majority of instances within higher education, that body is one of
the six regional accrediting agencies just examined. And although
all institutions under the jurisdiction of those six regional accrediting bodies must comply with the requirements related to assessment
and learning outlined earlier, the question becomes one of institutional transparency in communicating the results of those assessments, both internally and externally, and the extent to which those
assessments are actually used for institutional improvement and
quality enhancement. To illustrate the importance of planning and
assessment as cornerstones of institutional effectiveness, consider
the following statistics from the Middle States Commission on
Higher Education. Each year since 2001, about fifty-five to sixty
colleges and universities within the Middle States region go through
their decennial institutional self study. Within each cohort, about
60 percent of those institutions have been placed by the Commission on some form of follow-up activity—a progress letter or report,
monitoring report, and the like. And of those institutions requiring
follow-up activity, for about 80 percent the follow-up relates to
absence of full compliance with standards for assessment of student
learning outcomes, assessment of institutional effectiveness, and the
consistent use of assessment information to inform the institutional
planning process. Often it is a question not of providing evidence
that assessment is occurring, but rather of demonstrating in real,
tangible ways that the assessments are actually being *used* to inform
planning, decision making, and resource allocation at the institution. Comparable enforcement of related standards is found within
the other five regional accrediting bodies in the United States.

Institutional Responses to Calls
for Greater Transparency

After twenty years of steady criticism concerning the lack of
transparency at colleges and universities with regard to information

on student progress and general institutional operations, there has been movement recently among groups of colleges and universities to provide better information to external constituencies. Most notably, three higher education organizations—the National Association of State Universities and Land Grant Colleges (NASULGC), the American Association of State Colleges and Universities (AASCU), and the American Association of Colleges and Universities (AAC&U)—have collaborated to create a Voluntary System of Accountability (VSA). VSA is precisely what its name implies—a *voluntary* consortium of institutions providing a consistent set of prescribed data elements to meet external demands for greater institutional accountability and transparency. At this writing, private, independently chartered colleges and universities are in the process of developing a comparable reporting process. VSA provides participating institutions with a data template that requires them to provide current data on the following:

- Undergraduate profile (total headcount; breakdown by gender, ethnicity, age, and the like)
- Undergraduate success and progress rate (retention and graduation rates for specific cohorts of first-time freshmen and transfer students)
- Financial aid awarded to undergraduates, broken out by type or category of aid, such as grants, loans, scholarships
- Admissions profile, such as median test scores on the ACT or SAT, average high school grade point average
- Degrees awarded by level, and identification of top five fields of study at the institution
- Classroom environment—student/faculty ratio, data on class size
- Full-time faculty, by gender, ethnicity, and percentage with terminal degree
- Student housing—percentage of students living on campus

- Campus safety information
- Future plans of most recent cohort of baccalaureate recipients— employment, graduate school, volunteer service, military service, and so on

The template for reporting data, referred to as *The College Profile*, can be viewed at http://www.voluntarysystem.org/index.cfm. Although the foregoing data elements are interesting and instructive, they are hardly groundbreaking or innovative. Most higher education institutions with any sort of institutional research capability typically report these and other types of data on the institutional Common Data Set (CDS), a data template designed to enable institutions across the country to provide common information in response to seemingly endless requests for institutional information from college guidebooks, academic organizations, and other data consumers. And although VSA embeds the term *accountability* in its name, it is quite arguable that the data just outlined are not accountability data at all, but rather performance measures over which the institution has little control or that do not relate to student learning or institutional effectiveness in any meaningful or measurable way.

That said, VSA still brings greater transparency with respect to the measures it employs. It requires institutions to prominently indicate their participation in VSA and to provide a link to the VSA template on their institutional home page. The Common Data Set is frequently buried in the institutional research or other subpage on the institution's website, and it is up to the data consumer to find it. In contrast, if transparency regarding what is reported on the VSA template is a priority, VSA has ensured that its member institutions will make finding that template a fairly easy task.

To its credit, VSA is attempting to move institutions beyond simply providing descriptive data of the sort typically found in the Common Data Set. The VSA template allows institutions to describe how they evaluate the educational and social experiences of their students, and it encourages institutions participating in the National Survey of Student Engagement (NSSE), a broadly used standardized data collection instrument developed at Indiana University–Bloomington, to report results from selected items in that instrument, including but not limited to the percent of seniors who:

- Worked on class assignments and projects with other students
- Spent at least six hours per week outside of class on academic activities
- Used a learning lab or center to improve skills
- Would attend the same university again if they started over
- Had discussions with students whose race or ethnic background was different from their own
- Worked harder after receiving feedback from an instructor

The pattern evident in these items persists in the other NSSE items in the VSA template. They are interesting responses and may very well provide useful data to academic managers in shaping a better student experience at the institution. But they do not measure learning, and as such they do not address the transparency issue in that regard. To the extent that institutions have explicitly stated expected outcomes from encouraging students to (1) participate in group learning, (2) use out-of-classroom academic resources, or (3) understand and appreciate cultural diversity, NSSE is a useful tool in assessing the extent to which students are actually doing those things. But without knowledge of the institution's strategic goals and objectives in the area of student life and experiences, although the NSSE responses may be viewed as informative and instructive, they are self-reported and can hardly be categorized as "accountability data." Later in this volume, strategies will be presented for using data on student experiences to assess student life and student engagement as a component of overall institutional effectiveness and improvement.

VSA does give participating institutions an opportunity to describe strategies for assessing student learning outcomes at the course, discipline, and institutional level. But because there is no one-size-fits-all approach to measuring learning across the disciplines, descriptions of such assessment strategies can be cumbersome. Disciplines use various combinations of course-embedded test items, others capstone experiences, electronic portfolios, senior theses, and so on to describe learning, and the methodologies and qualifiers can appear outright confusing to those outside of higher education. These various approaches to measuring student learning, including their strengths and limitations, will also be discussed later in this volume.

To arrive at measures of core learning, VSA requires students at participating institutions to complete one of three standardized tests—the Collegiate Assessment of Academic Proficiency (CAAP), the Collegiate Learning Assessment (CLA), and the Measure of Academic Proficiency and Progress (MAPP). The use of standardized tests to measure general education skills does not currently enjoy widespread support in the higher education community, from either a conceptual or a methodological standpoint. Several instruments on the market purport to measure "critical thinking"—but what, precisely, constitutes critical thinking, and are the rubrics used to measure it across different instruments consistently measuring the same skills set? And assuming that all technical issues are addressed, there is still the human factor. Can we be sure that a group of several hundred students who are compelled to take a standardized test of several hours' duration, with no consequences in terms of either a grade or progress to a degree, will put forth their best effort in completing the instrument? Is this a legitimate measure of basic skills?

Although VSA has taken a commendable approach to providing institutional information to those outside of higher education, care should be taken in interpreting that information. Performance measures such as retention and graduation rates are not direct accountability measures. Many institutions—particularly two-year colleges—enroll students who are interested in specific courses but have no intention of obtaining a certificate or degree. Data on student engagement are self-reported by students and do not measure learning. Standardized test scores may measure learning, but with limitations on accuracy of the sort just noted. If an institution reports an average freshman score of 45 on the critical thinking portion of the Collegiate Assessment of Academic Proficiency, where scores can range from 40 to 80, what is that "45" really saying about freshmen at that institution? Or if seniors achieve an average analytic writing score of 1250 on the Collegiate Learning Assessment, compared with 1150 for freshmen, how does one interpret the score differential?

The core premise of this book is that, whether measuring learning or measuring the effectiveness and efficiency of human and fiscal resource deployment in support of teaching and learning, multiple measures are required, as well as multiple strategies for interpreting and communicating the results of those measurements. The book will focus on how institutions might best conceptualize what must be measured to frame a credible discussion of institutional effectiveness, what data collection tools are most effective in gathering those measures, and which analytical strategies are most effective in translating data into information that can be effectively communicated to both internal and external constituencies. And although a by-product of that credible discussion of institutional effectiveness may be a blunting of the sort of criticism directed at higher education that was described in this chapter, the primary intent in writing this book is to deliver a tool box to provosts, deans, department chairs, and administrative directors that will help them more effectively and efficiently manage their institutions. Specifically, the book will propose a broad cross-section of strategies and methodologies for assessing the full range of institutional operations at a college or university. And beyond that, the book will address the issue of how assessment data can best be translated into usable and useful information that informs the institutional planning process and provides the basis for making better decisions, particularly about the allocation of human and fiscal resources in support of activity related to student learning. In so doing, those institutions will indeed create a culture of evidence for institutional effectiveness that allows for greater transparency to external constituencies concerning the ways in which colleges and universities conduct their business.

2

STARTING AT THE BEGINNING

Mission-Driven Planning and Assessment

Any discussion of institutional effectiveness must look at a college or university's ability to effectively compete for the students, faculty, and staff that it has identified as central to its mission. In the book *Integrating Higher Education Planning and Assessment: A Practical Guide* (Hollowell, Middaugh, and Sibolski, 2006), published by the Society for College and University Planning, the authors argue that effective strategic planning focuses on four questions:

- Who are the institution's intended markets?
- What is the range of essential services needed to fully serve those markets?
- What is the most appropriate and effective institutional "branding" that will reach out to those markets?
- How will the institution know if it is successful in reaching and serving those markets?

The first two questions are at the core of institutional planning. To answer them with any degree of effectiveness, a college or university must first have a basic organizational philosophy that underscores what the institution values and what it aspires to be; in other words, a carefully drafted mission statement that anchors and provides context for strategic planning. The third question seeks strategies for effectively communicating that institutional mission to both internal and external constituencies, and the fourth question asks how best to *measure* the effectiveness of both planning and communication. This interrelationship between planning and measuring the efficacy of that planning—in other words, assessment of institutional effectiveness—is the central focus of this volume. Let's examine illustrative approaches to the four questions that guide planning.

The question of which constituencies an institution's markets comprise is a complex one, a question that colleges and universities should spend considerable time reflecting on. Because higher education institutions are multipurpose organizations, they serve multiple markets. Certainly the teaching component of an institution's mission implies that students are a central market for all higher education institutions, and indeed they are. But which students make up the student marketplace? More precisely, what is the mission-driven approach to admissions? Should the institution have some degree of selectivity in admitting students, and if so, how selective should it be? Or is an open admission policy more appropriate? And where there are students, so too must there be faculty and academic and administrative support staff. Once again, the mission-driven admissions policy will dictate the qualifications and skills that the institution seeks as it recruits faculty and staff, ranging from remedial activity to complex undergraduate research activity. But institutions frequently do more than teach. Research universities create new knowledge through pure and applied research and graduate student activity that is frequently the product of contract or grant partnerships with governmental and private entities. Most institutions have some measure of a service component that entails partnerships with state and local governments, community groups, public school districts, and the like. The effective institution has fully come to terms with its core mission, understands the multiple markets that it serves, has developed appropriate units to serve those markets, and knows how best to characterize or "brand" itself in reaching out to those markets. Let's move to a more detailed discussion of institutional mission as the primary driver for planning and assessment.

Institutional Mission

Before assessing its position within the broader marketplace, a college or university must first have a clear sense of purpose in approaching that marketplace. That clear sense of purpose should be fully articulated in the institution's mission statement. Each of the six regional accrediting agencies referenced in the previous chapter requires that member institutions have a written mission statement available to the general public that describes the essence of the institution. College and university mission statements are not public relations fluff—they should be carefully crafted statements about what an institution aspires to be, the values that it embraces, and its relationship with those outside of the institution. A good mission statement is devoid of cliché language such as "Students and faculty will interact in a rich intellectual environment in which each individual has the opportunity to achieve their full potential." This is a noble sentiment, but it tells us nothing of core institutional issues such as the balance between undergraduate and graduate education, the relationship between and among teaching, research, and service activity at the institution, and so on. Consider the following language in the University of Delaware's mission statement:

> The University reaffirms its historic mission to provide the highest quality education for its undergraduate students, while maintaining excellence in selected graduate programs. The faculty are responsible for helping students learn to reason critically and independently, gain knowledge of the diverse culture and environment in which they live, and develop into well-informed citizens and leaders. To accomplish these goals, the University provides a learning setting enriched by undergraduate student research, experiential learning, and study-abroad programs. The University places high priority on the education of qualified Delaware residents and provides

opportunity for a diverse group of citizens to participate in post-secondary education. Since the University is located in a state with a small population, providing programs of quality and diversity requires a community of student-scholars that reaches beyond the boundaries of the state, one that reflects the nation's racial and cultural diversity.

The University of Delaware also aspires to excellence in graduate education, the heart of which is scholarship and research. The creation, application, and communication of knowledge is a primary goal of the institution and of every faculty member, providing the substance for creative, informed teaching. Research is typically based on cooperation between faculty and students, whereby faculty mentors teach students to conduct independent research and to master problem-solving techniques. Through involvement of undergraduates in faculty research, the University creates a special bond between its undergraduate and graduate programs.

The University is also committed to providing service to society, especially in Delaware and the neighboring region. Public service is a responsibility of every academic unit. In addition, each faculty member is responsible for service to the University community and to his or her profession. The University emphasizes practical research, provides extension services, and works to solve problems confronting the community. (University of Delaware, 2001)

The nature of the undergraduate experience at the University of Delaware is clearly defined in the mission statement and helps to identify precisely which components of the admissions marketplace the institution will target, given its commitment to student scholars, qualified Delaware resident students, and a student body reflective of the nation's ethnic and cultural diversity. Equally clear is the relationship of undergraduate and graduate education with research and public service activity.

Community colleges are very different from research institutions such as the University of Delaware. That said, clarity of mission is no less important for two-year institutions. Consider the mission statement of Delaware Technical and Community College, which also serves the State of Delaware:

> Delaware Technical & Community College is a statewide multi-campus community college committed to providing open admission, post-secondary education at the associate degree level. The College offers comprehensive educational opportunities including career, general, developmental and transfer education, lifelong learning, workforce education and training, and community services. The College believes in the practical value of higher education as a means of economic and personal advancement. The College respects and cares for students as individuals and as members of diverse groups, and supports their aspirations for a better life. (Delaware Technical and Community College, http://www.dtcc.edu/effectiveness/pages/mission_statement.html)

The College translates its mission into the following summary academic policy:

> Delaware Technical & Community College is a statewide institution of higher education providing academic, technical, and corporate and community training opportunities to every resident of Delaware at four campuses throughout the state. The college is fully accredited and provides an open door, comprehensive program of education and training beyond high school. Over 100 degree, diploma, and certificate programs are offered in a variety of technical areas. Other offerings include GED certificates, workforce training for adults, industrial training for upgrading employee skills and youth programs. The college also offers various distance learning opportunities including telecourses, online courses, and interactive classroom courses. (Delaware Technical and Community College, http://www.dtcc.edu/future/)

Delaware Technical and Community College values open access and an open-admission process that requires only possession of a high school degree, which inherently defines an entirely different marketplace from that of a more selective institution such as the University of Delaware. And open access requires a different set of academic and institutional support services to meet the needs of an open admissions marketplace. The University of Delaware serves traditional, primarily residential 18- to 22-year-old undergraduates who enter the institution under a set of highly rigorous admissions criteria. As a result, the academic and student support services focus on enhancing already-well-developed intellectual skills and on using residence life as an extension of the academic experience to further develop social, aesthetic, and cultural opportunities that support general education objectives. Delaware Technical and Community College is a nonresidential institution that serves a substantial number of nontraditional students, many of whom require significant remediation in basic skills. Many of the College's students are adults seeking vocational training or retraining. The academic and student support services required by Delaware Technical and Community College students are centered on ensuring that students are college-ready, and they focus on support processes such as counseling, financial aid, and child care. Yet though the services at the University of Delaware and at Delaware Technical and Community College could not be more different in nature and in outcomes, each set of services is specific to the institution's mission and wholly appropriate to the markets it serves.

As colleges and universities define their markets and appropriate supporting services—academic, student, and institutional—it is important to simultaneously create an institutional "brand" that will speak to target markets. There are a number of fine examples of institutional branding. In the mid-1990s, the University of Delaware—a flagship state-related, land grant research university—wished to position itself in the admissions marketplace in a fashion distinct from other regional Land Grant universities such as Penn State University or the University of Maryland. Market consultants were brought in and immediately saw distinctive features at

Delaware that could be used to its advantage. In addition to nationally recognized honors and undergraduate research programs, and one of the oldest study abroad programs in the country, Delaware had a standing practice whereby even the most senior faculty were expected to teach at least one undergraduate course section per year. The consultants developed the branding tag line, "The University of Delaware—A Teaching University," and structured admissions viewbooks and other publications around that theme. The net result was that the university moved from 13,000 applications for 3,200 first-time freshman admission slots in 1995 to 24,000 applications for the same 3,200 seats a decade later.

Over in Trenton, New Jersey, a similar branding transformation took place in the 1990s. Trenton State College was part of the New Jersey System of State Colleges and Universities, along with Montclair State College, Richard Stockton State College, what was then called Glassboro State College, and others. In the 1990s, New Jersey sought to grow the system and provided funding incentives tied to enrollment. At the time when Montclair was transitioning from being a college to Montclair State University and Glassboro was becoming what is now Rowan University—indeed, it seemed like every former state college in the country was being renamed a university—Trenton State College took a different tack. Rather than grow the student body, Trenton decided to revise its admissions standards to become a highly selective, public liberal arts college—a bold decision, given that increased state funding was tied to enrollment growth, but one that clearly defined the mission of the institution. And Trenton changed its name to The College of New Jersey, setting it apart from the many neighboring Carnegie Masters institutions that were renaming themselves "universities." Its branding tag underscored the institution's mission-driven commitment to delivering the highest-quality liberal arts education to highly qualified undergraduates. It also engaged in a public squabble—ultimately resolved—with Princeton University over the name College of New Jersey, which had been part of Princeton's tradition at one time. The net effect of this strategy is that the College of

New Jersey is consistently ranked by U.S. *News and World Report's* "America's Best Colleges" in the top tier of public liberal arts colleges in the United States.

And perhaps the most classic example of defining a market niche and crafting a branding strategy to attract that niche is the University of Phoenix. From the outset, that institution never intended to compete with other universities for traditional 18- to 22 -year-old, residence hall–based college students. Marketing itself as "the University for Working Adults," it set up classrooms in rental facilities in major metropolitan areas across the country and created virtual twenty-four-hours-a-day, seven-days-a-week online course offerings in all of its disciplines. Reaching adults when and where they were able to engage in study, the University of Phoenix's success has been evident not only in terms of enrollment but also in terms of its results as a proprietary entity on the New York Stock Exchange.

It is the diversity of educational missions across colleges and universities that is one of the greatest strengths of American higher education. And it is that diversity of missions that poses the greatest challenge in assessing institutional effectiveness. There is no one-size-fits-all mission statement for postsecondary institutions, nor is there a one-size-fits-all set of measures for describing the degree to which colleges and universities are effectively meeting their missions. Yet the link between mission-driven planning and assessment of the effectiveness of that planning must be more than simply a philosophical construct for higher education textbooks. It must be a real component of best practices in the management of a college or university. The remainder of this volume will examine strategies for assessing how effective a college or university is in recruiting and engaging students, in meeting their academic and social needs, and in deploying the institution's human and fiscal resources in support of teaching and learning—*all within the context of the institution's specific mission.*

Before proceeding further, it will prove useful to look at a case study in which the linkage between planning and assessment was put into practice and was forged under particularly difficult institutional circumstances.

Linking Planning and Assessment: The University of Delaware

Hollowell et al. (2006), in their book *Integrating Higher Education Planning and Assessment: A Practical Guide*, provide detailed discussion of strategies for informing strategic planning activity with assessment information. Perhaps the clearest illustration of that linkage was highlighted in the case study they described with respect to planning activity at the University of Delaware during the decade of the 1990s. David Hollowell was executive vice president at the University of Delaware, and the author of this volume was assistant vice president for institutional research and planning. The circumstances underpinning the planning activity at the university so transformed the institution that it bears discussion here. The fact that planning and assessment have become so much a part of institutional culture at the university will be evidenced later in this chapter in a discussion of the findings of the decennial re-accreditation evaluation team that visited the institution a decade into the planning process.

Creating a Campus Culture for Planning and Assessment

Prior to 1987, management and planning at the University of Delaware could best be characterized as highly centralized and not terribly participatory. As recently as 1970, the university was a rather small institution of 7,500 students, primarily undergraduate, largely studying in the liberal arts. There was a smattering of graduate programs, primarily professional education and engineering. In the early 1970s the university's trustees decided that the institution should strive for flagship university status comparable to that of other major Land Grant institutions in surrounding states.

During the period from 1970 to 1985, the university grew from 7,500 students to over 20,000, adding substantial numbers of new programs at both the undergraduate and graduate levels. The decisions about how much to grow, and in which areas, were largely concentrated in the offices of the president and provost.

As is the case with many emerging institutions, rapid growth was followed by a period of stabilization and maturity. The president who oversaw the institution's growth retired in 1986 after nineteen years of service. His successor determined that the university needed to move from a highly centralized style of planning and management to a broadly participatory form of planning. In 1987, he launched a comprehensive strategic planning process, *Project Vision*, which entailed each academic and administrative unit on campus detailing where they expected to be in five and ten years, respectively, and the resources that would be required to get there. (Note: an important part of strategic visioning is defining the resource constraints that govern those visions; that did not occur here. The result was a compendium of "wish lists" that raised expectations in unrealistic ways.) It was a substantial undertaking, and it queried a broad range of constituencies on campus that had not previously been consulted with respect to the direction in which the university should move. One of the first by-products of this planning process was the university mission statement cited earlier in this chapter.

An unforeseen and unfortunate series of circumstances led to the abrupt resignation of the new president just over a year after he was hired. And just as he resigned, the fiscal price tag of the initiatives associated with Project Vision was tallied, and it was clearly prohibitive. The university moved into a period of uncertainty with respect to both leadership and the substantial investment of time and energy that had gone into planning activity. The former president who had presided over the growth during the 1970s agreed to return to lead the institution until a successor could be found.

Rather than lose the planning momentum that began with Project Vision, the returning president appointed a panel of senior distinguished faculty and asked them to take the Project Vision document and distill it into a road map that was more feasible from both a management and an affordability perspective. The latter qualifier was particularly important, as the Mid-Atlantic region where Delaware is located was entering a major economic recession. The result of the faculty panel's deliberation was a second planning document, *Focused Vision*, produced in the fall of 1989, at the same time that the university was appointing its twenty-fourth president, David Roselle.

When the new president arrived on campus, he immediately initiated a series of conversations with groups across campus representing every constituency of the university community, as well as alumni and local civic groups. The focus of the conversation was the identification of those initiatives in the Focused Vision document that were absolutely crucial to moving the university forward. Recall that the university's mission focused on the following:

> The University affirms its historic mission of providing the highest quality education for its undergraduate students, while maintaining excellence in selected graduate programs. . . .
>
> The University will continue to attract and retain the most academically talented and diverse undergraduate students, and support their intellectual, cultural, and ethical development as citizens and scholars.

As the president sought feedback on the institution's top strategic priorities, he required that any feedback be couched in terms of how a particular initiative *related to the core mission of the institution*. From the feedback he received, the president and his senior staff articulated four strategic areas in which the university would invest resources for the foreseeable future:

- *Competitive compensation for faculty and staff*: Any institution that is striving to provide the highest quality undergraduate and graduate education must be in a position to attract and retain the brightest young scholars in the nation as faculty, and similarly highly qualified professional and support staff to assist in providing a complete educational experience characterized by excellence.

- *Enhanced access to the university through increased financial aid:* The president committed the university to a policy that no student who demonstrated potential to succeed at the university at the level of intellectual rigor that the institution demands would be denied an education because of the inability to pay for that education.

- *A more student-centered campus:* Just as compensation is important to retaining the best faculty and staff, retaining the best and brightest students is contingent on providing essential student services and creating a campus climate that makes them feel welcomed and valued.

- *Providing state-of-the-art living and learning facilities:* Attracting and retaining both students and faculty can be done only when the facilities in which they teach and learn are appropriately equipped and aesthetically appointed in a fashion that supports the teaching/learning process.

How did the president arrive at these strategic priorities? The basic principle articulated throughout this book is that assessment must inform planning, and that was very much the case in developing these priorities. The prioritization of strategic initiatives was derived from a careful consideration of factual data describing university circumstances. Consider the following:

1. In looking at issues related to compensation, the University of Delaware compares its average faculty salary, by rank, with those at the twenty-four Category I doctoral universities (as defined by the American Association of University Professors) in the states contiguous to Delaware and in the District of

Columbia. This is done to ensure comparability with respect to cost of living. The relative position of the university among these institutions is annually monitored by the Office of Institutional Research and Planning. In 1990, the university ranked well in the bottom quartile among these institutions at each of the three major faculty ranks—full, associate, and assistant professor. Similar results for administrative compensation were seen through analysis of data from annual surveys done by the College and University Professional Association for Human Resources (CUPA-HR). The data suggested a strongly disadvantageous position for an institution seeking to attract and retain the best and brightest personnel available.

2. In 1990, the university routinely administered a locally developed survey, the College Student Selection Survey, that gathered information on the bases on which students make their college selection decisions. One of the categories was comparative financial aid packages. The university learned from successive administrations of this survey that, although the total dollar value of financial aid packages that the university was awarding was competitive with other institutions, University of Delaware packages were far too heavily weighted toward loans and work study funds, and were far too light on both merit- and need-based grants when compared with admissions competitors. Even the most naïve freshman understands the ramifications of student indebtedness and is most likely to attend the institution that offers the lightest debt load. The university was in a less than ideal position for attracting academically high-caliber students.

3. The university routinely administers the *ACT Student Opinion Survey*. For the sixty-two variables measuring student satisfaction, the university lagged behind the national benchmark for comparably sized institutions on twenty-seven, and exceeded the national benchmark on only twenty-one, being roughly equal on the remainder. These benchmarks, coupled with open-ended comments on the survey, provided clear evidence that students

found it difficult to access student services, and when they were successful they were often met with less-than-hospitable treatment from university employees. The data from multiple administrations of the Student Opinion Survey suggested that the university had considerable room for improvement in making students feel welcomed and valued—and that gap was hardly a recipe for attracting and retaining academically talented students who clearly have other options.

4. Examination of the university's Facilities Inventory indicated in 1990 that the cost to address the backlog of deferred maintenance at the institution exceeded $200 million. Any attempt to attract and retain the best faculty and students becomes highly problematic where living and learning facilities are substandard.

As the result of conclusions drawn from assessment information, in 1991 the president formally committed the university to the following goals:

- The university would be at or above the median *within five years* for average total compensation when measured against the standard twenty-four competitor institutions at each faculty rank. Staff would share in the same annual rate of salary increase given the faculty.

- The university would increase by 100 percent *within five years* the total volume of institutionally controlled financial aid.

- The university would see *within five years* statistically significant increases over the 1990 student satisfaction scores on the ACT Student Opinion Survey.

- The university would commit itself to a policy of annually setting aside *at least* 2 percent of the replacement value of the physical plant, to be used for building renewal and renovation. The rationale behind the 2 percent set-aside is that the projected life span of the typical academic facility is fifty years. Annually setting aside 2 percent of the replacement value of the physical plant means at the end of fifty years, sufficient funds are in place to replace the entire plant. The emphasis on "*at least*" acknowledged the magnitude of the deferred maintenance problem.

The question now became, how would the university pay for these initiatives? This was a particularly compelling problem given that the region was in the throes of an economic recession. The campus was informed that resource reallocation would be the mode for financing strategic initiatives until the economy enabled a normal growth in the institutional budget and the launch of the university's first comprehensive capital campaign. On what basis would resource reallocations be made? The president and his cabinet were committed to transparency in this regard, and they assured the institution that such decisions would be made on the basis of collegially developed assessments of productivity and effectiveness. A later chapter will describe strategies for administrative budget reductions and for the development of intra-institutional budget support metrics to underpin resource allocation and reallocation decisions between and among academic units. These budget support metrics drove resource allocation decisions that helped to fund the four strategic initiatives outlined by the president. In 1992, the university initiated the Delaware Study of Instructional Costs and Productivity to supplement and enhance the Budget Support Notebooks; strategies for using that tool are also described later in this volume.

In moving to a mode of resource reallocation, the university also made a public commitment to its students. The president acknowledged that higher education institutions have multiple revenue streams, and it was his intention to significantly diversify those revenue streams through increasing gifts, contracts, and grants. He indicated that there would be annual increases in tuition and mandatory fees, but to the greatest extent possible those increases would be held to a level comparable to the annual increase in the consumer price index. The strategic initiatives would be funded through increases in nontuition revenues and resource reallocation.

By 1995, the regional economy had sufficiently recovered to the point where the university launched the aforementioned capital campaign.

Once the president outlined his four strategic goals and accompanying timelines, the task of assessing the effectiveness of their implementation fell to the Office of Institutional Research and Planning. At regular intervals, each of the four initiatives was benchmarked—faculty and staff salaries in terms of position with respect to comparator institutions, financial aid in terms of annual percentage increase over the 1990 base, student centeredness in terms of gains in scores on the Student Opinion Survey, and facilities renewal and renovation in terms of reduction in the backlog of deferred maintenance. Reporting regularly and routinely on assessment of the effectiveness of implementing strategic initiatives was crucial to the success of the process. Academic and administrative units felt the pinch of resource reallocation, particularly in the early years prior to the capital campaign. Budget reductions within a given unit are more palatable if one can actually see salaries increasing, the quality of students improving as the result of use of scholarships as an effective admissions recruiting tool, greater student satisfaction as the result of improved business practices, and aesthetic enhancements to campus facilities.

Tangible Results of Planning and Assessment

It is useful to look at the outcomes for each of the four strategic initiatives from a decade-long perspective. That time frame encompasses not only the early years of resource reallocation but also the first five years of the capital campaign.

Faculty and Staff Salaries Table 2.1 displays the relative gains in average total compensation for full professors at the University of Delaware from academic years 1989–90 to 1999–2000. The university achieved its goal of being at or above the median for the comparator group, and it had done so by 1996. What is important in Table 2.1 is that in 1989–90, university compensation trailed that

Table 2-1   Comparative Gains in Total Compensation
(Total Compensation, 1989-90 Compared with 1999-2000)

FULL PROFESSOR

Institution	1989–1990		1999–2000
Princeton University	91,800	University of Pennsylvania	151,900
University of Pennsylvania	91,500	Princeton University	134,100
Georgetown University	88,700	Georgetown University	126,100
Carnegie-Mellon University	85,800	Carnegie-Mellon University	123,200
University of Virginia	85,100	University of Virginia	122,900
George Mason University	84,400	UNIVERSITY OF DELAWARE	116,200
Johns Hopkins University	83,800	Temple University	114,300
New Jersey Institute of Technology	83,100	George Mason University	113,900
Rutgers University - New Brunswick	82,000	College of William and Mary	113,400
Lehigh University	80,800	Lehigh University	111,300
University of Maryland - College Park	80,500	American University	111,100
Virginia Polytechnic Institute & State University	76,700	Johns Hopkins University	110,800
University of Maryland Baltimore County	76,700	George Washington University	110,800
University of Pittsburgh - Main Campus	76,500	New Jersey Institute of Technology	109,200
George Washington University	76,500	Rutgers State University New Brunswick	109,000
American University	76,300	Pennsylvania State University	108,600
Pennsylvania State University	75,300	University of Maryland - College Park	106,800
UNIVERSITY OF DELAWARE	74,700	University of Pittsburgh - Main Campus	105,600

(continued)

Table 2-1   (Continued)

FULL PROFESSOR

Institution	1989–1990		1999–2000
College of William and Mary	74,400	Virginia Polytechnic Institute & State University	103,800
Virginia Commonwealth University	72,600	Drexel University	103,700
Drexel University	71,000	Virginia Commonwealth University	103,300
Old Dominion University	70,400	University of Maryland - Baltimore County	96,200
Temple University	68,400	Howard University	93,300
Catholic University of America	64,800	Catholic University of America	86,800
Howard University	64,000	Old Dominion University	No report

Note: Per the Office of Institutional Research and Planning, January 1999, full professor salaries and total compensation are inflated by $1,500 to $3,000 at institutions with law schools as the result of inclusion of law faculty in the averages.

Source: ACADEME, Annual Salary Issues. Data for New Jersey Institute of Technology and Howard University were not reported for FY 1991; FY 1990 data were used in place of FY 1991 for those two institutions.

of seven other state-related institutions. By 1999–2000, only one state-related school, the University of Virginia, had higher total compensation for full professors. The same pattern holds for other faculty ranks and for staff salaries as well. The matrix in Table 2.1 was updated each year from 1990 on, and progression up through the comparative group was evident for each employee category.

Financial Aid Table 2.2 shows the growth in financial aid at the university. The important data element in Table 2.2 is university-administered funds; that is, those over which the institution has direct control. While the goal of doubling those institutionally

Table 2-2   Comparative Gain in Funding for Financial Aid

Growth In Undergraduate Financial Aid at the University of Delaware, FY 1990 Compared with FY 2000

	FY 1990	FY 2000	% Increase
University Administered Funds	$4,458,640	$28,036,660	528.8
State Grant Funds	$3,869,000	$6,643,500	71.7
Other Fund Sources	$2,169,602	$4,394,180	102.5
TOTAL	$10,497,242	$39,074,340	272.2

controlled funds by 1996 was achieved, what is remarkable is that over the course of a decade those funds had gone from $4.5 million to $28.0 million, more than quintupling. These dramatic gains were fueled in no small part by the capital campaign. Scholarships are a favorite category for donors. Needless to say, this growth provided leverage for increasing access to the university for the most academically qualified students. Again, the matrix in Table 2.2 was updated annually from 1990 on.

Student-Centeredness   Chapter Eight will speak of the need for simplicity in reporting survey results to nonstatistically savvy audiences. Table 2.3 illustrates the gains in student satisfaction scores on the ACT Student Opinion Survey over a five-year period. In reporting the scores, David Roselle, who holds a Ph.D. in mathematics and can run statistical circles around most data analysts, encouraged the most basic presentation of summary data from the Student Opinion Survey. A sports enthusiast, he suggested that the analysis focus on "wins," "losses," and "ties": a win when the university's score exceeded the national benchmark for a given variable, a loss when the university score lagged behind the national benchmark, and a tie when the two scores are within 0.1 of each other. He underscored that the important point was not to convey the statistical significance of differences between scores but rather to emphasize the magnitude of gains in student

Table 2-3   Comparative Gains in Student Satisfaction

Comparison of University of Delaware Scores on ACT Student Opinion Survey and National Norms

	1990 Scores Compared with National Norms	1995 Scores Compared with 1990 Scores	1995 Scores Compared with National Norms
University is ahead	21	44	39
University is tied	14	11	15
University is behind	27	7	8

Note: A "win" means the university's score exceeded the national benchmark for a given variable. A "tie" means the two scores are within 0.1 of each other. A "loss" means the university score lagged behind the national benchmark.

satisfaction. Table 2.3 is elegant in its simplicity in articulating those gains. The importance of translating data into understandable information and using it to effectively *communicate* assessment results will be underscored later in this book.

These student satisfaction gains reflected a position taken by the president and the executive vice president in 1991. For a May morning meeting, they assembled the directors of student services offices who reported to various vice presidents at the institution and told them, "As of today, you now report to the students." Their charge was to think of themselves as students and to develop a strategy for meeting student needs to ensure that a student would have to interact with at most one university employee, but under most circumstances would be able to address that need him- or herself. This creative approach to meeting student needs resulted in a new Student Services building that housed one of the first "one-stop shopping" operations in the United States. Students were able to register for courses; pay bills; and obtain transcripts, student identification cards, meal plans, parking permits, and so on, all in a single visit to the building. Student computer kiosks in the building enabled self-service in many instances. That this resonated with students is evident in the gains seen in Table 2.3. Subsequent administrations of the Student Opinion Survey saw those gains hold.

Facilities Renewal By 2000, the university had renovated every classroom in its entire building inventory, retrofitting most with state-of-the-art teaching technology. An aggressive program of fund raising enabled not only the aforementioned renovation and rehabilitation but also the construction of several new classroom and student services buildings. Over the course of a decade, the institution made substantial progress in moving from a significant backlog of deferred maintenance toward a program of planned maintenance.

In announcing the strategic goals, the president underscored the importance of their grounding in the university's mission. In 2001, when the university was visited by a Middle States Commission on Higher Education evaluation team following its decennial self-study, the team report concluded that:

> The University of Delaware has every reason to take enormous pride in what it has accomplished over the past 10 years. A decade ago, it was coming out of a period of considerable turmoil. Today, the University is seen as a national model for the integration of information technology in every aspect of University life: teaching and learning, research and service, academic support, and campus administration. It has created a physical plant that has few, if any, peers among public universities and would be the envy of most private colleges. These substantial achievements could not have happened without extraordinary leadership from the senior administration.

> Better than almost any University we are familiar with, Delaware has a clear sense of what it wants to be, namely, a University that offers high quality undergraduate education with targeted areas of excellence in graduate education and research.

> The review team was enormously impressed by the high level of morale that pervades the faculty, staff, and students. Almost without

exception, the people we spoke to take great pride in being part of the University. (Middle States Commission on Higher Education, 2001)

It is always refreshing to have institutional effectiveness validated by an objective third party.

It is worth mentioning that the clear progress in implementing the president's four strategic initiatives in the years prior to 1996, reported regularly in campus publications and alumni newsletters, helped pave the way for the university's capital campaign. Donors are actually investors in the institution's future, and investors are more likely to give money to an institution that is well managed and whose institutional effectiveness is clearly demonstrable along a broad range of measures. The capital campaign at the University of Delaware was launched in 1996 with a goal of raising $225 million. When the campaign concluded in 2002, $435 million had been donated. Demonstrable measures of institutional effectiveness are important not only to accrediting bodies; they also matter to potential donors.

Summary

The linkage between solid strategic planning and the comprehensive assessment activity that informs it is hardly unique to the University of Delaware. It is part of the institutional fabric of research universities such as The State University of New York at Albany and Syracuse University, of comprehensive institutions such as John Carroll University in Ohio and the University of Wisconsin at River Falls, and of community colleges such as Johnson County Community College in Kansas and Lehigh Carbon Community College in Pennsylvania. John Carroll University used effective strategic planning to reposition itself from a regional university with a limited market to a major liberal arts and professional education institution in the Midwest. The University of Wisconsin at River Falls, located a short drive from Minneapolis and St. Paul, took advantage of tuition reciprocity agreements between the states of Wisconsin and Minnesota to reposition itself as a higher education alternative for residents of the Greater Twin Cities. These are but a handful of examples of best practice in linking planning and assessment. The website of the Society for College and University Planning, www.scup.org, includes a rich set of resources that underscore this linkage. And the most effective means of learning about best practice is to contact campus representatives from those institutions that are most frequently cited as models for making highly effective planning decisions, grounded in information that has been systematically gathered to support institutional policy.

The foregoing discussion on planning and assessment at the University of Delaware focused on information that drove four specific strategic initiatives at that institution. The remainder of this volume will focus on assessment activities designed to gather information to support planning activity in the following broad areas:

- Students: prospective, enrolled, and alumni
- Faculty activity and productivity
- Administrative efficiency and productivity
- Effective and efficient use of financial resources
- Effective communication of information to support planning

Our discussion of assessing institutional effectiveness will begin in Chapter Three with an examination of issues related to students— the institutional choices that we make in admitting them, the ways in which we engage them, and the extent to which we meet their intellectual and social needs as a component of retention and completion. Chapter Four takes a look at the very special issue of measuring student learning outcomes as a core component of discussing institutional effectiveness. Chapters Five and Six will examine strategies for maximizing the effective deployment of human and fiscal resources within academic units to support teaching and learning; Chapter Seven will do the same with administrative units. As will be underscored throughout the book, assessment activity is meaningless unless the results of those assessments are used for planning and resource allocation decisions. Chapter Eight will focus on the most effective strategies for translating data into information that is likely to be used to enhance institutional effectiveness. And Chapter Nine will provide summary conclusions and a wrap-up to the discussion.

At every opportunity, the underlying rationale for collecting data will be tied back to the institutional mission. If there is a single takeaway message from *this* chapter, it should be the importance of institutional mission in framing strategic decisions at a college or university and in selecting the range and types of information that will be needed to make informed decisions.

3

ASSESSING INSTITUTIONAL EFFECTIVENESS

Student Issues

This chapter will focus on tools and strategies for measuring student attitudes and behaviors that are either directly or indirectly related to institutional effectiveness; that is, the ability of a college or university to fully achieve its mission. Let it be said at the outset that although we will examine specific data collection instruments and analytical strategies, these illustrative examples should not be viewed as endorsements of specific products. Rather, they exemplify how an institution might approach assessing specific mission-related issues. The choice of instruments and analytical approaches must be made in a fashion consistent with the resources and capabilities of each institution. This chapter is intended to spur exploration of the full range of assessment opportunities within specific areas of student life.

We begin the discussion of measuring institutional effectiveness by examining issues related to entering students. And although all students are important constituencies within the institutional marketplace, unless the institution has a particularly unique mission such as that of Rockefeller University or the Claremont Graduate Schools, where the focus is on postbaccalaureate education, undergraduates will make up the vast majority of its students, as they do in colleges and universities throughout the United States. Indeed, the most recent enrollment statistics posted on the website of the National Center for Education Statistics (http://nces.ed.gov/fastfacts/display.asp?id=98) indicate that 85 percent of students enrolled in degree programs in the United States are under-graduate. So the initial conversation in this chapter will focus on undergraduate students.

Let's say that an institution has developed a carefully articulated mission statement that clearly defines its admissions philosophy. That philosophical position translates into policy on admissions selectivity that can range from admitting only the most academically prepared applicants (for example, at Amherst College, Hamilton College, University of Virginia, University of North Carolina at Chapel Hill) to admitting largely first-generation college students, many of whom require academic assistance (such as at Delaware Valley College in Pennsylvania, Mercy College in New York State, University of the District of Columbia) to open enrollment institutions (such as at examples noted earlier: Delaware Technical and Community College, also community colleges in the state of California and the City University of New York system). Once the admissions philosophy is established, the question for the effective institution is how to attract students in the targeted market and, once they are enrolled, how to retain and graduate them.

Two-year institutions with a policy of open access, such as Delaware Technical and Community College, have defined their market as anyone interested in pursuing individual courses for personal or professional reasons, or those interested in pursuing a more formal course of study leading to a certificate or associate's degree. The issue for open access institutions, including four-year colleges that embrace that policy, is the articulation to potential students of the reasons why postsecondary education is important, and the programs and services in place at the institution that are designed to enhance academic success. To a certain extent, this is an "if you build it, they will come" market. There is a cadre of students who will attend an institution such as Delaware Technical and Community College to take advantage of access to associate degree and certificate programs, and coursework, for both transfer and vocational entry opportunities. These are academically well-prepared students who might well gain admission to a four-year institution, but for personal or financial reasons they elect to complete lower division study at the two-year college level before pursuing upper division study at a senior institution, often through an articulation agreement between the two institutions. But there is a second cadre of students at open access institutions who are less academically prepared and for whom intervention and remedial services will prove critical to academic success. In examining student services, student satisfaction with those services, and the total pattern of student engagement at the institution, it is important to use institutional mission as a filter in examining data related to those dimensions.

For institutions with specific admissions standards, the competition for qualified students can be intense, and the strategies for assessing the institution's effectiveness in competing for students are crucial. Because multiple institutions are competing within the same pool of potential applicants, it is important that institutions be strategic in mining that applicant pool. Commercial vendors such as the College Board's Enrollment Planning Service (EPS) provide institutions with tools for identifying admission prospects, for tracking students from the point of expression of interest through the actual application process, and for assessing cross-applications and cross-admissions in determining which institutions are actually admissions competitors and the extent to which they compete. It is critically important that selective admission institutions understand who their competitors are in order to more effectively develop their own institutional "brand" and thus more effectively reach targeted potential applicants. Quantitative tools such as those provided by the Enrollment Planning Service enable institutions to numerically see to which other institutions our applicants are applying, which other institutions are offering admission, and to which institutions they are losing students to whom they have extended an offer of admission. These issues are important not only to four-year institutions but also to two-year institutions such as Brookdale Community College in New Jersey or Johnson County Community College in Kansas, where substantial numbers of students enroll in associate in arts and associate in science degree programs with the specific intention of, on receipt of the associate degree, transferring to a four-year institution to complete baccalaureate studies. In these instances, two-year and four-year institutions are competing for the same students.

Other quantitative information is crucial to effective management of the admissions component of enrollment planning. The overall size of the student body at any institution is generally a function of the capacity of academic space on campus combined with pedagogical decisions with respect to optimal class size. Once these determinations are made, factors such as attrition and retention rates and time-to-degree analyses on cohorts of entering first-time students help to shape the target size of those first-time student cohorts. Suppose an institution has a first-time freshman target of 3,400 students for the fall semester. The effective institution will rely on history to manage admission activity in the pursuit of that 3,400-student target. Specifically, the institution will need to know the following:

- Based on historical yield rates (the number of students offered admission who actually attend the institution), how many offers of admission must be made in a given year to produce 3,400 first-time freshmen?

- Based on historical patterns, how many applications must the institution receive to arrive at the desired number of admissions offers without compromising academic standards? Clearly, the greater the number of applicants, the more selective the institution can be.

To effectively manage these variables, an institution must be able to monitor where it is within a given admissions cycle against comparable points in prior admissions cycles. Table 3.1 displays a weekly monitoring report that looks at three years of admissions data for the second week in September. A similar report would have preceded this one for each week in the admissions cycle, usually commencing around the first week in October.

Table 3-1   Eastern Seaboard State University Weekly Admissions Monitoring Report

Campus Summary: First-Time Freshman Applicants, by Admission Status and by Residency Status for the Entering Classes in the Fall of 2005 as of 09/15/05; Fall 2006 as of 09/18/06; and Fall 2007 as of 09/13/07.

	Resident	Nonresident	Total
All Applicants			
2005	2,340	18,984	21,324
2006	2,332	19,209	21,541
2007	2,088	20,133	22,221
Admission Denied			
2005	109	7,506	7,615
2006	148	5,871	6,019
2007	172	5,838	6,010
Admission Offered			
2005	1,940	7,295	9,235
2006	1,877	8,101	9,978
2007	1,747	8,489	10,236
Admission Accepted			
2005	1,362	2,078	3,440
2006	1,255	2,201	3,456
2007	1,174	2,348	3,522
Ratio of Offers to Total Applications			
2005	0.83	0.38	0.43
2006	0.80	0.42	0.46
2007	0.84	0.42	0.46
Ratio of Accepts to Offers (Yield)			
2005	0.70	0.28	0.37
2006	0.67	0.27	0.35
2007	0.67	0.28	0.34

The weekly admissions monitoring report is a baseline administrative assessment that allows institutions to make midcourse corrections in the offer rate, based on the number of applications, to ensure that the target entering class size is met. Similarly, looking at yield rates over time enables the institution to more intelligently focus on adjusting offer rates and marketing efforts directed at expanding the applicant pool, both within the context of the institution's mission.

As useful as the quantitative information is within the admissions monitoring report template, the critical information that a college or university needs from an institutional effectiveness point of view is a fuller understanding of why students who have been extended an offer of admission to our institution choose to go elsewhere. How is our institution perceived by admitted students compared with actual admissions competitors? Compared with institutions we aspire to compete with? How do students acquire information about our institution? What is the role of teachers, guidance counselors, parents, friends, and college guidebooks in the process? How effective are the institution's admissions materials? For institutions seeking to effectively compete in the admissions marketplace, these are critical questions. And they are questions for which answers can and must be obtained.

In the late 1970s and 1980s, as competition for students became more intense, many institutions developed locally prepared surveys to provide answers to the questions just raised. The author of this volume created such an instrument, The College Student Selection Survey, in the late 1970s while employed in the State University of New York system and used it over the course of the next decade, sharing it with other institutions interested in similar research. It was modified in 1985 for use at the University of Delaware (see Appendix A). During the 1990s, the College Board developed the Admitted Student Questionnaire (http://professionals.collegeboard. com/higher-ed/recruitment/asq), generally abbreviated to ASQ, which fully addresses a set of questions similar to those in The College Student Selection Survey, but is administered and analyzed by the College Board. It is superior to "home-grown" instruments because of its capability for extensive benchmarking. The capacity to compare activity within a focal institution with that at actual and aspirational peer institutions, as a characteristic of highly effective institutions, will be a recurring theme throughout this book. It is not surprising, then, that the call for benchmarking begins with the college admission decision. The ASQ provides participating institutions with a rich base of information on such dimensions as these:

- College characteristics
- Colleges to which a given student has applied, and a rank ordering based on preference of those to which the student was admitted
- Sources of information about colleges
- Financial aid packaging (need-based and merit-based grants, loans, work study, and so on) at focal institution and comparators

There are two versions of the ASQ—the standard version, and the ASQ Plus, which provides institutions with detailed comparisons with up to five selected peer institutions. We will use ASQ Plus to describe the information that the ASQ provides to an admissions office, although similar but not identical information can be gained from the standard version of the ASQ. The instrument provides a listing of sixteen institutional characteristics, ranging from academic reputation to availability of majors and special academic programs to quality of facilities, and so on. Respondents are asked to indicate how important each of the characteristics is in shaping the college selection decision. Respondents are then asked to evaluate and compare those characteristics at the focal institution and the next two "top choice" institutions, by name, to which the student was admitted. The data derived from this exercise are extraordinarily useful. Exhibit 3.1 displays a standard analytical matrix provided by the ASQ Plus, in this instance for a hypothetical institution.

Exhibit 3.1 provides a college or university, its admissions office, and marketing personnel with a concise snapshot of where the institution stands vis-à-vis the competition on those characteristics that drive the student's choice of a college. In this instance, the fact

Exhibit 3.1 Importance and Rating of Selected Institutional Characteristics

A. *Less Important and the University Rated Higher*	B. *Very Important and the University Rated Higher*
Special academic programs	Attractiveness of campus
	Cost of attendance
	Value for the price
	Quality of social life
	Availability of recreational facilities
	Extracurricular opportunities

C. *Less Important and the University Rated Lower*	D. *Very Important and the University Rated Lower*
Access to off-campus activities	Academic reputation
Prominent athletics	Personal attention
	Quality of on-campus housing
	Undergraduate teaching commitment
	Surroundings
	Quality of academic facilities
	Availability of majors

Note: "Characteristics Considered Very Important" were those rated "Very Important" by at least 50 percent of respondents. "Characteristics for Which the University was Rated High" were those for which the mean rating of the University was higher than the mean rating for all other institutions. The characteristics are listed in decreasing order of the difference between the mean rating for the University and the mean rating for all other institutions.

that the focal university is rated lower than the competition on access to off-campus activities and prominence of athletics is not a matter of concern, as these issues were rated of lesser importance by those completing the ASQ. On the other hand, issues such as academic reputation, personal attention, commitment to undergraduate teaching, and availability of majors should be of major concern, as these are factors rated very important in the college selection decision, and the focal institution is rated lower than the competition.

A common institutional response to a portrait such as that in Exhibit 3.1 is that the respondent pool simply does not know (1) the academic rigor of the institution, or (2) that all undergraduate students have access to senior faculty, or (3) that the range of majors in the undergraduate catalog is extensive. Even if that is the case, when viewing and analyzing ASQ data we must keep in mind that *prospective student impressions need not be accurate to be real.* Effective institutions must come to terms with the reality of perceptions within the admissions marketplace. An institution that fully grasps the significance of the information in Exhibit 3.1 will capitalize on the institution's current position with respect to attractive tuition and the perceived value received for price paid. At the same time, it will develop appropriate institutional policies for addressing real shortcomings in the lower right quadrant of Exhibit 3.1, while cultivating marketing strategies to correct misperceptions. An important piece of information that both the ASQ and the ASQ Plus provide is the source or sources of information that students use to learn about an institution—parents, friends, guidance counselors, view books, college guides, or others—and whether the information provided is favorable or unfavorable. This information is essential when thinking about marketing strategies targeted at changing student perceptions about the institution.

The ASQ Plus provides a listing of descriptors (such as "prestigious," "fun," "selective," "back-up school," "challenging") and asks respondents to use the descriptors to characterize the focal school and the same two top choice competitors as in the previous analysis. Table 3.2 draws on that information to show how our hypothetical university is viewed by enrolling students compared with those who chose to attend another institution. Once again, the perceptions of non-enrolling students need not be accurate to be real. The data in Table 3.2 suggest that the focal institution has some room for work on its image if it hopes to attract the population to whom it has extended an offer of admission, but who choose to attend elsewhere.

Often, the college selection decision comes down to money, and it is imperative for an effective institution to know where it stands in comparison with the competition in the area of financial aid

Table 3-2   Impressions of the University Among ASQ Respondents

	All Admitted Students	Enrolling Students	Non-Enrolling Students
College Images N (%)	2545 (100%)	1530 (100%)	1015 (100%)
Fun	61%	68%	50%
Friendly	57%	63%	47%
Comfortable	53%	61%	41%
Large	41%	43%	39%
Highly Respected	41%	50%	27%
Partying	40%	41%	38%
Intellectual	36%	45%	23%
Challenging	34%	43%	21%
Athletics	30%	34%	26%
Career-Oriented	30%	38%	17%
Selective	29%	33%	23%
Prestigious	28%	35%	16%
Diverse	26%	29%	22%
Personal	19%	23%	13%
Average	13%	7%	22%
Back-Up School	12%	5%	21%
Difficult	9%	12%	4%
Isolated	6%	2%	11%
Not Well Known	6%	4%	8%

Note: Boldfaced traits are those more likely to be important to how an institution is perceived.

packaging. The ASQ provides respondents with the opportunity to compare the aid package offered by the focal institution with those offered by the two top-choice institutions used in the other analyses. Table 3.3 displays the information that can be culled from the ASQ.

Table 3.3 indicates that, when compared with competing institutions, the focal institution tends to be substantially lighter in grant aid than the competition, hence the overall aid package is lower than those offered by competitors. For long-term strategic

Table 3-3   Comparative Financial Aid Packages from Admitted Student Questionnaire

	Average Aid Awarded by Focal School (Enrolling Students)	Average Aid Awarded by School Attended (Non-Enrolling Students)
Students Reporting Work-Study Awarded		
N	89	79
Average Award	$2,045	$2,107
Students Reporting Loan Awarded		
N	316	193
Average Award	$3,948	$4,915
Students Reporting Need-Based Grant Awarded		
N	143	104
Average Award	$4,310	$9,354
Students Reporting Merit Grant Awarded		
N	301	218
Average Award	$7,180	$12,024
Students Reporting Total Aid Awarded		
N	482	297
Average Award	$8,281	$16,011

planning purposes, this information is crucial to effective institutions seeking to attract those students who are currently opting to attend other colleges or universities. Highly effective institutions will use these data as the focus for activity within a capital campaign, or as the basis for reallocating existing resources. Competitive financial aid packages are essential to effective admissions recruiting activity, and analyses of the sort gleaned from the ASQ Plus provide critical information in assessing an institution's position within the financial aid marketplace.

Table 3-4 Average High School Grades of ASQ Respondents

	All Admitted Students	Enrolling Students	Non-Enrolling Students
Average High School Grades N (%)	1664 (65%)	1011 (66%)	653 (64%)
A (90 to 100)	76%	72%	82%
B (80 to 89)	24%	27%	18%
C (70 to 79)	0%	1%	0%
D (69 or below)	0%	0%	0%

The ASQ also provides important demographic information about enrolling and non-enrolling students. Although comparable information can be obtained from other sources, such as the Enrollment Planning Service, it is useful to have information that is specifically reflective of the respondents to the ASQ. An example of the type of information that can be gathered is seen in Table 3.4.

Serious research that defines an institution's position in the admissions marketplace is essential to attracting those students who constitute the focus of the institutional mission. Whether an institution is seeking students with high-end academic preparation or first-generation students who require additional academic assistance, it is important for the institution to know whether it is reaching its target audience, how it is perceived by that audience, which institutions constitute the major competition for the target audience, and the dynamics of the student college selection decision within that market. Whether an institution uses a commercially prepared instrument such as the Admitted Student Questionnaire or a home-grown survey is a matter of choice and resources. The important issue is that the research gets done on a systematic and regular basis to inform the institution of the extent to which it is achieving its admissions recruiting objectives.

Once students are admitted, it is important to fully understand the range of programs and services that will be required by first-time freshmen and transfer students. Although high school and transfer college transcripts provide a good portrait of the academic capabilities of entering students, the student needs that effective institutions must address frequently go beyond the classroom. The effective institution can employ at least two strategies in gathering this information.

ACT Evaluation Survey Services (http://www.act.org/ess/) provides a broad range of commercially prepared data collection instruments to assist colleges and universities in assessing various dimension of institutional effectiveness. Among these is the College Student Needs Assessment Survey. Typically administered in the summer before new students enter college or in the weeks immediate following their arrival, the survey addresses various issues confronting them as they enter the institution.

In the section titled "Career and Life Goals," the College Student Needs Assessment Survey asks students to assign the level of importance in their life to twenty specific goals—such items as "have a steady, secure job," "be recognized as an expert in my field of study," "own and operate my own business," and "help others who are in need." Their responses inform the institution how much the entering students are driven by specific life objectives, and the areas in which those objectives lie. The range of the twenty career goals and objectives listed in the survey instrument is sufficiently diverse to give institutions a reasonable assessment of the extent to which entering students are learning-centered, career-oriented, introverted/extroverted, and holistic in their approach to life. Because colleges and universities are interested in educating the whole person, profiles of this sort can be useful in shaping both academic and student support and social opportunities at the institution.

The meat of the College Student Needs Assessment Survey is titled "Educational and Personal Needs"; it encompasses fifty-eight different areas in which students may potentially require assistance. These include items related to choice of academic major or area of study; financing a college education; enhancing study skills, oral and written communication, and quantitative, technological, and library skills; time management; and general preparation for life and civic engagement. Students are asked to estimate the extent of help they feel they will need in each area, using a scale that ranges from "a lot" through "a medium amount" and "a little" to "none." The depth and breadth of this fifty-eight-item inventory of student needs provides a rich base of information for tailoring academic and student support services to enhance prospects for student success. A number of creative institutional assessment offices opt to administer the College Needs Assessment Survey at the end of the first year at the institution, rephrasing the items to determine how much students feel that the institution provided the level of assistance they required in each area of need. Whether an assessment office opts for the ACT instrument or another commercially prepared survey, it is important to get a sense of entering student needs to ensure that appropriate strategies and services are in place to enhance student satisfaction and engagement upon enrollment.

A second approach to gathering information from students entering an institution is Indiana University's College Student Expectations Questionnaire (CSXQ). This instrument was adapted from the widely used College Student Experiences Questionnaire (CSEQ), which was also the precursor of the National Survey of Student Engagement (NSSE), both of which will be discussed shortly. All three instruments address the quality of the student experience at a college or university. In the case of the CSXQ, it speaks to the anticipated experience from the perspective of the entering student.

Within the area titled "College Activities," the CSXQ asks students how often they expect to engage in specific activities related to a number of dimensions of college life including library and information technology, experiences with faculty, course learning, reading and writing, campus facilities, extracurricular activities, interaction with other students, scientific and quantitative experiences, topics of conversation with faculty and students, and so on.

Additionally, the CSXQ asks students the extent to which they anticipate that the campus environment will emphasize scholarly, intellectual, and practical skills and how helpful and supportive they expect various offices and personnel on campus to be throughout their collegiate careers. The attractive feature of the CSXQ is that the content of many of the items is identical to that of items on the CSEQ. Consequently, it is possible to correlate expectations with actual performance once the student has actually spent time engaged in the campus environment. As was the case with assessing entering student needs, it is important to have an accurate sense of entering student expectations with regard to the academic environment at the institution and the extent to which those students hope to actively engage with that environment.

Summing up pre-enrollment assessment of student issues, for a college or university to be effective in the admissions marketplace, it must have a clear sense of mission with respect to the students that it hopes to attract. In reaching out to those students, the institution must have a distinctive "brand"—that is, a posture that sets it apart from competitors in the marketplace. To ensure that the branding is effectively reaching those for whom it is intended, market research such as that done through the Admitted Student Questionnaire or a locally prepared instrument is essential to understanding both how the institution is perceived by prospective students and the dynamics of their college selection decision. Once students have been admitted, it is equally important to understand the academic and social needs of entering students as well as their intellectual and interpersonal expectations of campus climate and opportunities for student engagement. Student satisfaction and engagement have repeatedly been highly correlated with student retention and graduation. Creating an effective and successful process for ensuring student success does, indeed, begin before those students spend their first day in class. The assessment process will have already been well under way.

Developing Usable Measures of Student Engagement and Satisfaction

Pascarella and Terenzini, in the 2005 update of their classic work *How College Affects Students*, examined thirty years of research on factors that impact student achievement and student success. Starting with Astin's (1985) assertion that students learn by becoming more involved, Pascarella and Terenzini (2005) summarize that research to arrive at the following unambiguous conclusion: "Other things being equal, the strongest evidence indicated that the greater a student's engagement in the academic work or the academic experience of college, the greater his or her level of knowledge acquisition and general cognitive growth" (608). They go on to suggest that this student engagement takes the form of student effort in mastering the rigor of course content; the quality of interaction with faculty, both in and out of the classroom; how much students interact with peers in collaborative learning and social settings, especially those from different backgrounds; the extent to which students are exposed to a variety of curricular content including service-learning and ethical education components; and so on. It is clearly important that institutions provide structured opportunities for such a variety of student engagement; of equal importance is student satisfaction with the number and quality of such opportunities.

Measuring Student Engagement

The University of Delaware appointed Patrick T. Harker as its twenty-fifth president in July 2007. A central policy focus for President Harker, as outlined in his strategic planning document, *The Path to Prominence*, is a diverse and stimulating undergraduate academic environment that actively engages students in a broad range of intellectual pursuits. He characterizes it as follows:

> The University of Delaware must attract students who bring brilliance, talent, life experiences, and diversity—ethnic, geographic, and

socioeconomic—that are characteristic of great universities. A University of Delaware education will ensure that intellectual curiosity and a passion for learning become habits of mind. Our students must have opportunities for innovation, entrepreneurship, and creativity. We must also enrich our students beyond the classroom with shared experiences and traditions that bind them to the University and to each other and create pride in their alma mater.

Over the next decade, we will remain close to our current undergraduate enrollment, focusing on continuing improvement in student qualifications for success rather than on increasing student numbers. Diversity is an increasingly important dimension of educational quality as our students prepare for success as leaders in the global community. Accordingly, incoming University of Delaware classes will become increasingly diverse—ethnically, culturally, regionally, internationally, and intellectually. (Harker, 2008, 5)

How can the University assess its success in creating the intellectual climate just described and in engaging its undergraduate population in meaningful ways? Fortunately, there is a substantial body of research and survey instrumentation in support of measuring student engagement.

Some of the earliest research on the quality of student effort in college centered around the work done by C. Robert Pace at the University of California at Los Angeles, using the College Student Experiences Questionnaire (CSEQ). As noted earlier, Pace's research indicated that "the more the student is psychologically engaged in activities and tasks that reinforce and extend the formal academic experience, the more he or she will learn" (Pascarella and Terenzini, 2005, 119).

The CSEQ (http://cseq.iub.edu/) is a comprehensive data collection instrument that can yield a wealth of information on the extent of student effort and involvement in a broad range of educational activity. The CSEQ begins by collecting standard background information, including variables that may relate to the quality of student effort, such as the number of hours per week spent working at a job, whether or not the individual is a first-generation college student, and whether the student has easy access to a computer. The main body of the survey focuses on a series of grouped activities that characterize the collegiate experience and asks respondents to indicate how often they have engaged in each of those activities, using a four-point scale ranging from "very often" to "never." These activities are listed in Exhibit 3.2. In addition to assessing the extent and quality of these types of activities, the CSEQ collects data on the number of books and articles read and the number and lengths of papers written during the academic year. Students are also asked to assess the academic rigor at the institution along a number of general education dimensions also listed in Exhibit 3.2. Having asked students to assess institutional emphasis on specific general education competencies, the CSEQ closes by asking respondents to estimate the extent to which they have progressed and made substantive gains in specific skills and behaviors directly related to those general education competencies.

It should be noted that the CSEQ is available in two versions, directed at four-year and two-year institutions. From the perspective of assessing institutional effectiveness, the CSEQ is a marvelous resource in indirectly measuring student learning through the respondent self-estimate of cognitive gains in specific general education competencies, and in describing the impact of the collegiate environment in developing those competencies. It should also be noted that the assessment dimensions listed in Exhibit 3.2 clearly reflect the emphases earlier outlined in the University of Delaware's strategic initiative emphasizing a more engaged undergraduate student body. And that emphasis is hardly unique to Delaware; it is an educational objective that most colleges and universities—public and private, four-year and two-year—embrace. Consequently, the CSEQ would seem to be a perfect measurement tool.

In a perfect world, that would be the case. But we live in an imperfect world. Over the past decade, institutional research offices

Exhibit 3.2   Assessment Dimensions in the College Student Experiences Questionnaire (CSEQ)

How Often Do Respondents Engage in the Following Activities:

Library: Examines the extent of use of library facilities and engagement in discrete library skills such as use of indices or data bases to retrieve information, develop bibliographies, etc.

Computer and Information Technology: Measures the extent of student use of the computer to write reports, use of e-mail as a communication tool, use of the Internet as an information gathering tool, use of the computer for statistical analysis, etc.

Course Learning: Measures the extent to which students engage in specific course-related activities such as completing assignments, taking notes, contributing to class discussions, working collaboratively with other students on a class project, etc.

Writing Experiences: Assesses student use of tools such as dictionary, thesaurus, writing style manual. And the extent to which the student seeks assistance from faculty or others in writing clearly, etc.

Experiences with Faculty: Examines the extent of various student interactions with faculty, including discussion of courses, academic advising, career counseling, out-of-classroom discussions, formal undergraduate research activity, etc.

Clubs and Organizations: Assesses the extent of student involvement in extracurricular organizations and activities of various types, etc.

Personal Experiences: Assesses the extent and quality of various types of personal interactions between and among students, faculty, and staff, and the extent to which students seek formal and informal assistance with personal matters, etc.

Student Acquaintances: Measures the extent and type of interactions with students from different belief/value systems, ethnic and national backgrounds, etc.

Scientific and Quantitative Experiences: Examines the extent to which students engage in specific activities related to mathematics, science, laboratory experiences, use of scientific method, etc.

Topics of Conversation: Examines the extent to which students engage in conversations concerning a broad range of topics including current events, social issues, different lifestyles and mores, arts, science, politics, etc.

(continued)

Exhibit 3.2 (Continued)

How Often Do Respondents Engage in the Following Activities:

Art, Music, Theater: Measures student engagement in the arts through frequency of taking painting and/or music courses, visiting a gallery or museum, attending a concert or recital, participating in orchestra, chorus, or dance, etc.

Campus Facilities: Measures the extent of use of various campus buildings and facilities for intellectual, social, cultural, and athletic activities, etc.

Information in Conversations: Assesses the impact of conversations on students in terms of the extent to which they use knowledge acquired in class, are stimulated to do further reading on the topic, or are persuaded to change an opinion as the result of the conversation, etc.

Respondent Assessment of Institutional Academic Rigor:

- Institutional emphasis on developing academic, scholarly, and intellectual qualities
- Institutional emphasis on developing aesthetic, expressive, and creative qualities
- Institutional emphasis on developing critical, evaluative, and analytical qualities
- Institutional emphasis on developing an understanding and appreciation for diversity
- Institutional emphasis on developing information literacy skills
- Institutional emphasis on developing vocational and occupational competence
- Institutional emphasis on the personal relevance and practical value of coursework

and other administrators of student surveys have observed a sharp decline in response rates. This is due in part to "survey fatigue" on the part of students who receive countless questionnaires from multiple sources over the course of an academic year. Students are disinclined to complete paper surveys, preferring web-based instruments. Students are also disinclined to complete lengthy surveys, and the downside to the CSEQ is its length. Because it is so comprehensive, it is eight pages long, and there is an inverse relationship between the length of a survey and its completion rate. Although the CSEQ is available in a web-based version that somewhat increases the likelihood of completion, it is important to carefully plan the survey administration to include follow-up contact with the study sample, to underscore the importance of the survey information to institutional academic planning, and to again encourage participation and completion of the survey. Where successfully administered, the CSEQ yields a wealth of information related to the quality of the student experience on a given campus. As such, it is an invaluable resource for identifying and enhancing activities and opportunities for students that, indeed, lead to greater engagement—which, as the research has consistently demonstrated, is highly correlated with student retention and academic success.

When the project's founder, C. Robert Pace, retired, administration of the CSEQ was moved to Indiana University in Bloomington, where Pace's colleague, George Kuh, was director of the Center for Postsecondary Research. In 1998, Kuh, with the full cooperation of Pace, commenced development of the National Survey of Student Engagement (http://nsse.iub.edu/index.cfm), usually shortened to NSSE, which was based on the CSEQ and supported by a grant from The Pew Charitable Trust. Available in both paper and web-based format, the NSSE has developed stable measures of validity and reliability. Unlike the CSEQ, which is typically administered to a sample of students across the four years of undergraduate study to assess general student patterns of engagement, the NSSE was created initially to collect data from freshmen and seniors, and to measure difference in engagement early and late in the academic career. Although the NSSE can be administered to sophomores and juniors at the institution's request, the analytical focus for the NSSE at the national level continues to be differences between freshmen and seniors with respect to types and levels of student engagement, and self-reported intellectual and social gains as the result of that engagement. It should also be noted that there is a two-year version of the instrument, the Community College Survey of Student Engagement (CCSE). More fully involving students in a broad range of academic and co-curricular activity is as important in the two-year sector as in the four-year institutions.

The analytical foci of the NSSE are listed in Exhibit 3.3. In looking at those analytical dimensions, the evolution of the NSSE

Exhibit 3.3   Assessment Dimensions in the National Survey of Student Engagement (NSSE)

Level of Academic Challenge: Examines the extent to which students prepare for class, the quantity of course readings and papers written, course skills and content emphases, campus academic skills and content emphases.

Student Interactions With Faculty Members: Measures the extent to which students discuss assignments, grades, career plans with faculty, engage in student-faculty research, interact with faculty outside of the classroom, etc.

Supportive Campus Environment: Assesses the extent to which students feel that the institution provides resources to enable them to succeed academically, to cope with nonacademic issues, that foster a nurturing social environment, and that foster constructive relationships between and among students, faculty, and staff.

Active and Collaborative Learning: Measures the extent to which students ask questions and contribute in other ways during class, make class presentations, work collaboratively with other students on class projects, tutor peers, engage in community-based projects, and discuss course-related ideas outside of class.

Enriching Educational Experiences: Examines the extent to which students interact with others of a different race or ethnicity, with different religious and political beliefs, different opinions and values; the extent to which the campus environment encourages contact among students of different economic, social, racial, or other ethnic backgrounds; the extent to which the institution emphasizes the use of technology; and the extent of student participation in a wide range of activities including internships, community service, study abroad, independent study, senior capstone experiences, co-curricular activities, and learning communities.

---

from the CSEQ is clearly evident. The advantage of the NSSE over the CSEQ is its shorter length and the buy-in from participating institutions seeking to develop clear, descriptive information on student growth over the course of an academic career. Although the scope of the NSSE is ambitious and akin to the CSEQ, the Center for Postsecondary Research at Indiana University—home to the NSSE—has demonstrated over the past decade that it can successfully collect, analyze, and report out high-value data to participating institutions. And participation has been robust, growing from 276 institutions in 2000 to 774 institutions in 2008. The NSSE provides participating institutions with analytical results for each survey item for their own students; equally important, it provides benchmark data from other participating institutions based on criteria such as geographic proximity to the focal institution, comparable Carnegie institutional classification with the focal institution, and groupings of peer colleges and universities chosen by the focal institution.

When institutional data reports arrive from the NSSE, they contain a wealth of information that initially appears daunting and poses something of a challenge with respect to communicating information to nonstatisticians. It will be a recurring theme throughout this volume that data are not necessarily equivalent to information, particularly when dealing with numbers-phobic audiences. Presenting data tables so dense with numbers that they come close to making the eyes bleed is hardly an effective form of communication. In presenting NSSE data—or any other data related to institutional effectiveness on which decisions can and should be made—it is important to clearly understand what it is that needs to be communicated, and develop the simplest, most user-friendly communication strategy possible. The old maxim, "A picture is worth a thousand words"—or in this instance, a thousand numbers—frequently applies.

One of the most attractive features of the NSSE is the ability to benchmark institutional responses with appropriate comparator groups. The NSSE Report provides mean benchmark scores for all participating institutions falling within the same Carnegie

Institutional Classification as the focal institution. The NSSE also allows institutions to define a second peer grouping by selecting its own subset of schools from the participant pool. Figure 3.1 graphically depicts comparison data for the University of Delaware that assesses the extent to which students at the institution write papers that require the integration of ideas and information gathered from different sources.

At the University of Delaware, the NSSE information is conveyed to end users via two different charts. The first compares the most recent administration of the NSSE with that immediately preceding it, in this instance the 2005 administration compared with that of 2001. The average scores for freshmen and seniors on each of the two administrations are compared. In Figure 3.1, it is readily evident that both freshmen and seniors in 2005 report somewhat fewer instances of writing integrative papers than was the case in 2001. The second chart compares the 2005 freshman and senior responses with the two peer groups provided by the NSSE. The first is made up of participating Research Universities, as defined by the Carnegie Taxonomy, whereas the second comprises institutions that the University of Delaware has identified as actual and aspirational peers. This comparison is important in that the 2005 score differential for University of Delaware freshmen was determined to be statistically significantly lower than the mean score for either peer grouping, suggesting an area of general education that the institution may wish to monitor to see if the pattern persists or worsens in subsequent survey administrations. Figure 3.2 displays similar comparisons with respect to the amount of time spent preparing for class. It should again be emphasized that simply assessing student engagement is not sufficient. The crucial activity focuses on what is actually *done* with the assessment information. At the University of Delaware, the NSSE data, in part, provided the basis for a reexamination by the Faculty Senate of the basic constructs of the general education curriculum and the strategies used to assess general education competencies across the disciplines.

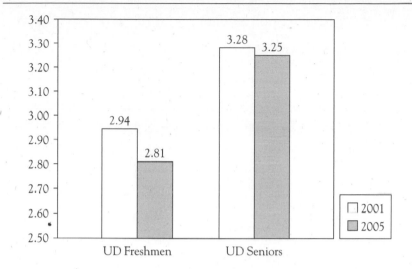

Note: Both 2005 freshmen and seniors worked on projects requiring integration of ideas and information less frequently than in 2001. 2005 University of Delaware freshmen fall statistically significantly below their counterparts at both national research and peer universities on this measure.

1 = Never; 2 = Sometimes; 3 = Often; 4 = Very Often

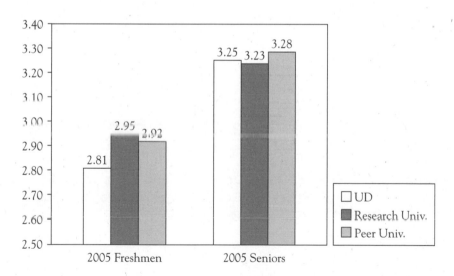

Figure 3.1 How Often Have You Worked on a Paper That Required Integrating Ideas or Information from Different Sources?

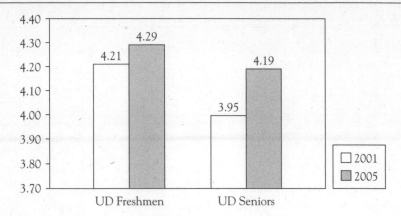

Note: 2005 University of Delaware freshmen and seniors both spend more time preparing for class than was the case in 2001. The 2005 University of Delaware responses for freshmen and seniors are not statistically significantly different from those at national research and peer universities.

1 = 0 Hrs/Wk; 2 = 1-5 Hrs/Wk; 3 = 6-10 Hrs/Wk; 4 = 11-15 Hrs/Wk; 5 = 16-20 Hrs/Wk; 6 = 21-25 Hrs/Wk; 7 = 26-30 Hrs/Wk; 8 = More Than 30 Hrs/Wk

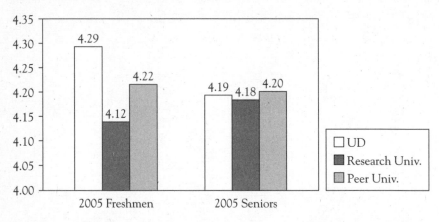

Figure 3.2 How Much Time Do You Spend Each Week Preparing for Class (Studying, Reading, Writing, Rehearsing, and so on)?

The important concept in the Figure 3.2 reporting template for the NSSE data is the visual simplicity of the information being conveyed. A brief statement summarizing the findings, with an indication of statistical significance where appropriate, makes it easy for the reader to digest both the intra- and interinstitutional comparisons. Dense, data-packed tables frequently discourage the reader from engaging with the information those data may convey. As noted earlier, a picture is a quick and powerful way of ensuring that the message will be absorbed.

The Center for Postsecondary Research at Indiana University has developed companion instruments for both the NSSE and CCSE. The Faculty Survey of Student Engagement (FSSE) has institutional faculty examine the same dimensions of student engagement that are assessed through the NSSE and CSSE, and to evaluate the extent to which the faculty member sees students as engaged. Faculty may opt to make this determination either for the population of students in their individual classes or as a judgment about the "typical" student at the institution. The end result of data analysis from the FSSE should be more than simply a comparison of the convergence or divergence of student and faculty assessments of student engagement along a particular dimension. It should also provide faculty with a quantitative basis for shaping a conversation about areas in which students could indeed be more fully engaged and for developing learning strategies to achieve that end.

A similarly useful tool is the Beginning College Survey of Student Engagement (BCSSE), which is administered to entering students and gathers information on precollege academic and co-curricular activity. Taking a different tack from that of the College Student Needs Assessment Survey cited earlier in this chapter, which asked students to self-identify the areas of academic and social college life in which they might need assistance, the BCSSE asks students about their actual involvement and engagement in discrete academic and social dimensions of high school life as a means of identifying those areas where students clearly have not been as engaged as they could have been. Such dimensions include analytical thinking, effective writing, use of technology, working effectively with others. Not surprisingly, these dimensions are virtually identical to those assessed through the NSSE. Taken together, the BCSSE and NSSE enable identification of engagement gaps prior to entering college, and the extent to which those gaps are closed during the college experience.

The issue of student engagement is so important to student retention and success that the Center for Postsecondary Research at Indiana University has encouraged the development of consortia of NSSE users to develop and disseminate models of best practice. Project DEEP (Developing Effective Education Practices) is a collaboration between the NSSE Institute—which is housed at Indiana University and is the developer of the survey instrument—and the American Association for Higher Education, directed at disseminating information related to student engagement practices that resulted in higher-than-predicted graduation rates at twenty participating institutions. The results from this project can be viewed on the NSSE Institute website at http://nsse.iub.edu/institute/index.cfm?view=deep/overview. And two-year institutions widely share CCSE data through the National Community College Benchmark Project, housed at Johnson County Community College in Kansas, which benchmarks not only student engagement data but also a host of other student measures related to institutional effectiveness. A full description of the project is found at http://www.nccbp.org/.

Measuring Student Satisfaction

As important as student engagement is to active learning, so too is there a strong correlation between student satisfaction with the institutional environment and persistence to degree. Pascarella and Terenzini note that, "Rewarding encounters with the formal and informal academic and social systems of the institution presumably lead to greater student integration in these systems and thus to persistence" (2005, 54). Thus student satisfaction research is a cornerstone of enrollment management at an effective college or university.

Although many institutions opt to develop their own student satisfaction surveys, locally prepared instruments lack the capability of benchmarking institutional scores on various dimensions of satisfaction with those from appropriate peer groups. Two commercially produced instruments—the Noel-Levitz Student Satisfaction Inventory and the ACT Student Opinion Survey—enjoy widespread use and merit some discussion here. Each of the instruments assesses student satisfaction with programs and services offered by the institution, as well as characteristics of the campus environment. Both offer versions of the survey specifically tailored to two-year and four-year institutions, respectively.

The Noel-Levitz Student Satisfaction Inventory (https://www .noellevitz.com/Our+Services/Retention/Tools/Student+Satisfaction+Inventory/) instruments are designed to assess twelve scales that contribute to an assessment of student satisfaction. For each item in each scale, the student rates both the importance of that item and the extent of satisfaction.

*Noel-Levitz Student Satisfaction^{TM} Scales**

- Effectiveness of Academic Advising
- Campus Climate
- Campus Support Services
- Concern for the Student as an Individual
- Instructional Effectiveness
- Admissions and Financial Aid Effectiveness
- Registration Effectiveness
- Responsiveness to Diverse Populations
- Campus Safety and Security
- Excellence Campus Services
- Student Centeredness (attitudes toward students)

The Noel-Levitz provides participating institutions with a highly useful report containing national benchmarks for each of the items

*These labels are not exactly as described by Noel-Levitz. © Copyright 1994, Noel-Levitz, Inc. Reprinted with permission. This material may not be posted, published, or distributed without permission from *Noel-Levitz, Inc.*

in the Student Satisfaction Inventory. The report contains a strategic planning overview that identifies institutional strengths (those items with high importance and high satisfaction scores) and institutional challenges (high importance and low satisfaction scores), as well as a benchmark report that compares institutional satisfaction scores with the national mean for participating institutions, both overall and within each of the scales assessed on the survey. Institutions using the Noel-Levitz have a clear road map for identifying both areas that would be appropriate to emphasize in student recruiting materials as well as other areas of strategic importance that require attention. Philadelphia University in Pennsylvania has made particularly effective use of Noel-Levitz data in reengineering its student services as it grew and transitioned from its former identity as the Philadelphia College of Textiles to become a full-fledged comprehensive university. In growing the size of the student body across new curricular areas, and in introducing a more substantial residential component, it was critical for Philadelphia University to be able to continuously monitor the extent to which it was meeting critical student needs and to be able to make those assessments within a comparative context of how other institutions were performing. The Noel-Levitz Student Satisfaction Inventory provided the institution with the appropriate instrument and analyses for those circumstances.

ACT offers service similar to Noel-Levitz with respect to their Student Opinion Survey. That instrument asks students to indicate whether they have used, and how satisfied they are with, specific programs and services typically found at a college or university. For example, the four-year version of the Student Opinion Survey asks students to assess their satisfaction with the following:

- Academic Advising Services
- Personal Counseling Services
- Career Planning Services
- Job Placement Services

- Recreational/Intramural Programs
- Library Facilities and Services
- Student Health Services
- Student Health Insurance Program
- College Tutorial Services
- Financial Aid Services
- Student Employment Services
- Residence Hall Services
- Food Services
- College Social Activities
- Cultural Programs
- College Orientation Program
- Credit-by-Examination Program
- Honors Program
- Computer Services
- College Mass Transit Services
- Parking Facilities and Services
- Veterans Services
- Day Care Services

The fact that students indicate whether or not they actually used a given service enables filtering of the data such that satisfaction scores provided by students who did not use the services can be recoded to missing data.

The Student Opinion Survey also asks students to rate their level of satisfaction with forty-three aspects of a typical college or university environment. The items are organized as follows:

1. *Academic:* for example, course content in major field, instruction in major field, out-of-class availability of instructors, value of information provided by advisor.

2. *Admissions*: for example, general admissions procedures, accuracy of information received before enrolling.

3. *Rules and Policies*: for example, student voice in college policies, rules governing student conduct, personal security and safety.

4. *Facilities*: for example, classroom facilities, study areas, student union, general condition of buildings and grounds.

5. *Registration*: for example, general registration procedures, availability of desired courses at times student can take them, billing and fee payment procedures.

6. *General*: for example, concern for the student as an individual, attitude of college nonteaching staff, racial harmony on campus, campus media.

Both the Noel-Levitz Student Satisfaction Inventory and the ACT Student Opinion Survey give participating institutions the opportunity to develop additional, institution-specific optional questions for inclusion in the survey (twenty items on the Noel-Levitz, thirty items on the ACT). This feature is useful for drilling down further on standard items on the survey or for addressing issues that are not included in the standard areas on the surveys.

As with the Noel-Levitz survey, the ACT provides a set of national benchmarks that display the mean national score for each item on the Student Opinion Survey, arrayed on the basis of the following institutional demographics:

- Institutional Control (public; private)
- Type (four-year; two-year)
- Size (under 2,000 students; 2,000 to 6,000 students; 7,000 or more students)
- Class (freshmen and sophomores, grouped; juniors and seniors, grouped)
- Gender (male; female)

- Age (twenty-five and under; twenty-six and over)
- Ethnicity (Caucasians; all minorities, grouped)

The broad array of institutional demographics allows partici-pating institutions to analyze student satisfaction within subgroups of strategic importance to that college or university.

In presenting the Student Opinion Survey data (or Noel-Levitz data), it is important to remember that the vast majority of those viewing the analysis are not statistically savvy. Most experienced institutional researchers have watched audience eyes glaze over almost immediately on hearing terms such as "confidence interval" or "one-tailed or two-tailed test of significance." The important principle here is to convey *information*, not simply present data. And in such instances, as stated earlier, a picture is worth a thousand numbers. Figure 3.3 displays actual data from a recent administra-tion of the Student Opinion Survey at the University of Delaware. Both of the charts in Figure 3.3 display differences that are statistically significant, as noted. And that is the end of the statistical discussion; the emphasis is on information. Clearly, most institu-tions participating in a student satisfaction survey welcome instan-ces in which the institutional score is significantly higher than the national benchmark (in this instance, for institutions with total enrollment of seven thousand or more students), particularly on a critical student satisfaction variable such as out-of-classroom availa-bility of instructors. At a major research institution such as the University of Delaware (with an undergraduate enrollment over fifteen thousand), access to course instructors is an essential component not only of academic success, but also in making students feel valued as individuals.

There are, however, instances in which a student satisfaction score that is significantly lower than the national benchmark is not a bad thing; it may actually reflect the effectiveness of the institution. The second chart in Figure 3.3 reflects student satisfaction with rules concerning student conduct. In the months prior to this

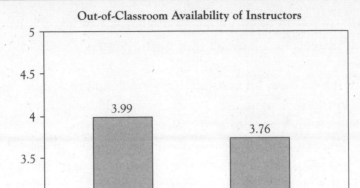

Out-of-Classroom Availability of Instructors

Note: Difference is statistically significant.

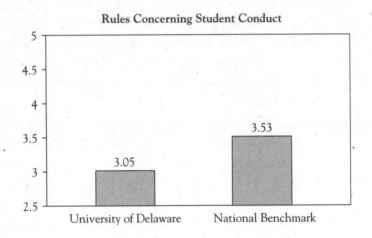

Rules Concerning Student Conduct

Note: Difference is statistically significant.

Figure 3.3 Representative Charts from Student Opinion Survey Analysis

particular administration of the Student Opinion Survey, the University of Delaware had instituted a "three strikes" policy with respect to underage consumption of alcohol, under which parents were notified of the first two offenses and the student was asked to leave the University following the third offense. The Student Opinion Survey allows for open-ended comments, and it was evident from those comments that the University's alcohol policy was a major source of dissatisfaction.

What Can the Data Tell Us About Student Retention and Attrition?

To comply with federal requirements with respect to graduation rates for first-time freshmen, most institutional research offices use one methodology or another directed at examining cohort survival over time. Table 3.5 displays just one such analysis. For each cohort from fall 2001 through fall 2007, under the heading "Enrollment and Dropout Rates," persistence and dropout rates are displayed, indicating the percentage of those students who entered in the initial fall term that returned the following and subsequent fall terms, and the percentage who left without graduating after those fall terms. Under the heading "Graduation Rates," the percentage of the entering cohort graduating within four, five, and six years and beyond is displayed for each respective group of entering first-time freshmen.

Cohort survival analyses are essential to modeling enrollment forecasts. Knowing historical persistence and graduation rates, coupled with time-to-degree analyses, enables institutions to forecast, with a reasonable degree of confidence, the percentage of current entering first-time freshmen who will be lost at specific points in time. From this data, we can make reasonable forecasts of student course demand, tuition revenue, and other important variables. The quantitative data relating to student tracking, seen in Table 3.5, are crucial to achieving those ends. However, what the cohort survival table in Figure 3.1 does not indicate are the underlying reasons why some students persist to graduation, whereas others leave without obtaining a degree.

Research on the reasons why students leave an institution without graduating is often highly problematic. Yet such information is

Table 3-5 Retention and Graduation Rates for Seven Cohorts of First-Time Freshmen

| | | Enrollment and Dropout Rates | | | | | Graduation Rates | | | |
| | 1st | 2nd | 3rd | 4th | 5th | 6th | Within 3 yrs | Within 4 yrs | Within 5 yrs | Total |
Entering Fall Term	Fall	Fall	Fall	Fall	Fall	Fall				
2001 N	3545	3080	2830	2762	653	118	22	2079	2621	2727
% Enrollment	100.0%	86.9%	79.8%	78.5%	18.4%	3.3%	0.6%	58.6%	73.9%	76.9%
% Dropout	0.0%	13.1%	20.2%	21.5%	22.9%	22.7%				
2002 N	3513	3126	2871	2757	526	83	31	2193	2632	2684
% Enrollment	100.0%	89.0%	81.7%	79.4%	15.0%	2.4%	0.9%	62.4%	74.9%	76.4%
% Dropout	0.0%	11.0%	18.3%	20.6%	22.6%	22.7%				
2003 N	3128	2738	2524	2453	496	85	24	1884	2297	–
% Enrollment	100.0%	87.5%	80.7%	79.2%	15.9%	2.7%	0.8%	60.2%	73.4%	
% Dropout	0.0%	12.5%	19.3%	20.8%	23.9%	23.8%				

Year											
2004	N	3358	2976	2746	2674	472	0	31	2138	–	–
	% Enrollment	100.0%	88.6%	81.8%	80.6%	14.1%	0.0%	0.9%	63.7%	–	–
	% Dropout	0.0%	1.4%	18.2%	19.4%	22.3%	0.0%			–	–
2005	N	3399	3055	2866	2787	0	0	42	–	–	–
	% Enrollment	100.0%	89.9%	84.3%	83.2%	0.0%	0.0%	1.2%	–	–	–
	% Dropout	0.0%	0.1%	15.7%	16.8%	0.0%	0.0%		–	–	–
2006	N	3433	3035	2808	0	0	0	–	–	–	–
	% Enrollment	100.0%	88.4%	81.8%	0.0%	0.0%	0.0%	–	–	–	–
	% Dropout	0.0%	1.6%	18.2%	0.0%	0.0%	0.0%	–	–	–	–
2007	N	3442	3064	0	0	0	0	–	–	–	–
	% Enrollment	100.0%	89.0%	0.0%	0.0%	0.0%	0.0%	–	–	–	–
	% Dropout	0.0%	1.0%	0.0%	0.0%	0.0%	0.0%	–	–	–	–

absolutely critical to effective enrollment management. Students rarely signal their intention to leave; they vote with their feet. Exit interviews capture only a small proportion of nonpersisting students. Conducting surveys of withdrawing and nonreturning students is often frustrating. These require correct student addresses, and even where those are in hand, the response rate to such surveys is usually quite low among a population that has no stake in replying. And exit interviews and withdrawing or nonreturning student surveys usually yield one or both of two politically correct reasons for leaving: personal or financial circumstances.

A number of institutions have taken a different approach to researching the reasons why some students persist and others leave. It entails a modest modification of the approach to student satisfaction research. At such institutions, the ACT Student Opinion Survey (any other satisfaction survey would work equally well) is typically administered during the spring term to a robust random sample of students cutting across the freshman, sophomore, junior, and senior classes. Care must be taken to oversample those segments of the student body with historically low response rates. During the following fall term, the survey respondent pool is disaggregated into two groups:

- Those who took the survey in the spring and returned to the institution in the fall
- Those who took the survey in the spring and did not return in the fall and did not graduate

The satisfaction scores on each survey item from the two groups are then examined for statistically significant differences in response patterns.

The results of such an analysis are often stunning. Those students who know in the spring that they are not returning to the institution, but who have not openly signaled that intention, are often brutally candid in their survey responses. As the result, institutions are able to focus on areas of substantial discontent among nonreturning students. As an example, two such areas at the University of Delaware in 2003 through 2005 were academic advising and registration.

Simply knowing the areas of discontent is not sufficient. Further drill-down is essential. The University of Delaware developed a series of "Campus Pulse Surveys," short, web-based data collections that focus on specific topical areas uncovered through student satisfaction research. The information gathered with respect to academic advising resulted in the restructuring of the advising program at the institution to ensure that students, particularly freshmen and sophomores, had access to trained academic advisors with a full understanding of the needs of new college students. The registration survey yielded different information. The institution had implemented a new registration system using distributed web-based software that is substantially different from the older mainframe-based software. The clear pockets of discontent centered among students making the transition from old to new software and procedures. Younger students who had experienced no other environment were quite content with current software and procedures. Rather than spend substantial money modifying the software, energy was focused on assisting those students (and faculty, for that matter) who were encountering difficulty with the procedures, knowing that in time we would have a student body far more comfortable with the current environment. Other Campus Pulse Surveys have yielded equally useful information, and the process is easily implemented at any institution.

Alumni Research

Effective institutions continue to monitor the ongoing relevance of the college or university experience of graduates beyond the receipt of a degree. Institutions typically survey samples of alumni graduating classes at regular intervals—most often in five-year cycles—to determine whether employment is curriculum related, whether graduate school followed baccalaureate education, and other types of information that help academic planners gauge the relevance of institutional curricula to postgraduate life. There is often a second reason for engaging in alumni research, related to prospect development for annual development activity and capital campaigns. Unfortunately, the central purpose of alumni research—whether it concerns the relevance of the college or university experience or is preparation for fund raising—often becomes murky to the point where the alumnus just assumes it is another subtle pitch for money and discards the instrument.

There is an abundance of both commercially developed and institutionally created alumni survey instruments that suit both of the institutional needs described earlier. One need only enter "alumni survey research" into any internet search engine to retrieve countless examples. (Indiana University-Purdue University at Indianapolis offers a particularly good example of alumni research.) The important point is that clarity in the purpose of the research is critical. A letter from the campus president or provost soliciting alumni participation should be very clear on why the institution is reaching out to its graduates. If information on how the college or university has prepared its students for postgraduation life is the objective, be clear on that purpose and make it clear that the information gathered here is for use in academic planning, not for the Development Office. On the other hand, prospect research among alumni is becoming increasingly important as other revenue sources diminish. Surveys designed for that purpose should include a cover letter that makes the case for dependency on alumni contributions and an instrument that measures the variables important to such an endeavor—alumni income, employer matching, and the like.

Alumni can be a wonderful source of information about the ongoing effectiveness of a college or university education. And they can also be a valuable revenue stream in institutional finances. However, to achieve any sort of useful response rate it is very important to separate the different roles of alumni research. Where student engagement and student satisfaction—as measured through the aforementioned assessment strategies—are high, alumni are more likely to be engaged in responding to either type of alumni research.

Summary

This chapter has presented a broad array of tools and strategies for assessing the extent to which a college or university is effectively meeting its mission through recruiting students from targeted markets, and academically and socially engaging those students in ways that enhance student satisfaction with the college experience, increasing the likelihood of retention and completion. The literature on student engagement and learning and on student satisfaction and persistence clearly document that, in each instance, the more that the former are present, the more evident the latter will be. Highly effective institutions take this information to heart and design appropriate assessment strategies to determine the extent of student engagement and satisfaction, then *use* those assessments to convey information that enables strategic planners to enhance both engagement and satisfaction.

4

A CORE ISSUE IN INSTITUTIONAL EFFECTIVENESS

Developing Sensible Measures of Student Learning

Although this book focuses on strategies for assessing institutional effectiveness, no college or university can be considered effective unless it can demonstrate that its students are learning. The teaching/learning process is at the core of higher education, and the intent of this chapter is to briefly review strategies related to assessing student learning.

As discussed in Chapter One, over the past two decades institutions of higher education have had to respond to cascades of criticism about their effectiveness in producing academically qualified graduates. For years, the focus at colleges and universities was on teaching effectiveness. Strategies such as student evaluations of teaching and faculty peer assessments of teaching were employed to determine whether the individual in the front of the classroom was effectively disseminating the core content in a given academic course. And while the focus was on the effectiveness of the faculty member in teaching, little attention was paid to whether students were actually learning. Faculty members stood at the podium in large lecture halls, dispensing treasure troves of information to a roomful of students who, it was assumed, were diligently taking notes and, like good sponges, soaking up all of the wisdom being proffered in their direction. At the end of the course, the student was assigned a course grade with the presumption that the grade was a sufficient and satisfactory measure of the extent to which the student had mastered the course content. The problem was that employers and other consumers of higher education's graduates found skill levels that did not match the grades on the college transcript—hence the public outcry.

The criticism of the way higher education measured student success was not solely external. In 1976, Paul Dressel, a faculty member in the School of Education at Michigan State University, offered the following tongue-in-cheek characterization of course grades: "[Grades are] . . . an inadequate report of an inaccurate judgment by a biased and variable judge of the extent to which a student has attained an undefined level of mastery of an unknown proportion of an indefinite material" (Dressel, 1976, 2). While humorous, the characterization is not far off the mark for too many courses. Course grades are, at best, imprecise calibrations of student performance that are influenced by numerous intervening variables. Grades can be affected by factors such as student motivation and effort, and willingness and ability to meet organizational norms (Pascarella and Terenzini, 1991). Put bluntly, grades can be affected by the extent to which students regularly attend class, the extent to which they actively participate in class, and their verbal ability reflected in that participation. The criteria for student performance that constitutes an "A" in Physics 101 is likely different from that for Philosophy 101. And within Physics 101, ten different sections taught by ten different graduate teaching assistants are very likely to have different calibrations for the difference between an A and B student performance. In other words, an A in one course is not necessarily the same measurement of student performance as an A in another course.

This is not to say that grades are totally unreliable assessments of student learning. Higher education has arrived at a point where it acknowledges that grades are not the sole measure of student learning. A comprehensive assessment of cognitive gains among students at a college or university requires *multiple* measures and *multiple* pieces of evidence. This approach to measuring student learning has been codified into the accreditation standards of the member institutions in each of the six regional accrediting bodies across the United States.

What Are Accreditors Looking For?

As an example of the parameters of a good protocol for assessing student learning outcomes, consider Standard 14 in the Middle States Commission on Higher Education's *Characteristics of Excellence: Eligibility Requirements and Standards for Accreditation*, which reads as follows:

> Assessment of student learning demonstrates that, at graduation, or other appropriate points, the institution's students have knowledge, skills, and competencies consistent with institutional and appropriate higher education goals. (2006, 63)

Although the wording of the standard may appear to be fairly benign, the institutional requirements under that standard are quite substantial. What are the fundamental elements of assessment of student learning that the Middle States Commission on Higher Education (2006) seeks from its member institutions?

1. Clearly articulated statements of expected student learning outcomes at all levels—course, degree/program, and institution—and for all programs that aim to foster student learning and development. These expected student learning outcomes must be:
   • Appropriately integrated with one another;
   • Consonant with the institution's mission;
   • And consonant with the standards of higher education and of the relevant disciplines. (66)

Crafting statements of expected student learning outcomes within these guidelines requires careful thought. As the outcomes that describe expected acceptable student performance in Math 101 are developed, care must be given to how those outcomes articulate with the broader expected learning outcomes that will be manifest in graduates with an undergraduate or graduate degree in mathematics. And those outcomes for mathematics graduates must be clearly tied to the expected student learning outcomes for *all* graduates of the institution, often expressed in terms of general education skills.

It is important to note that student learning outcomes are expected to be *consonant with the institution's mission*. As was discussed in Chapter Two, there is rich diversity in the missions of institutions that constitute higher education in the United States. And just as there is diversity in the level of academic preparedness of entering students consistent with the stated mission of an institution, so too is there diversity in the expected student learning outcomes. Certainly, in crafting quantitative skills outcomes for a freshman class in mathematics, the expected student performance measures at an open-admission community college catering to first-generation college students ought to be very different from the expected student performance measures at an Ivy League university. That said, it is incumbent on both institutions to demonstrate that, at graduation, students leave the institution equipped with collegiate-level mathematical skills.

It should also be noted that the standard for assessing student learning requires clearly articulated statements of expected outcomes from *all* programs that aim to foster student learning and development. To the extent that units such as the Division of Student Life or the Division of Residence Life are engaged in student developmental activity on a campus, they must create, implement, and measure specific expected outcomes from their activity. Counseling services, career planning services, student activities centers, and the like clearly fall into this category. Many institutions have living/learning programs in residence halls, organized around specific general education skills developed by the institution. Accreditors would expect to see formal statements of expected outcomes from these programs, as well as appropriate metrics that measure the extent to which those outcomes are being achieved among students involved in those programs.

Note that throughout this discussion, the emphasis is on *students*—plural, not singular. Assessment of student learning is about aggregate student performance, not the performance of an individual student. And it is about cognitive gains across course sections and across academic disciplines. As such, it is also not about the performance of an individual faculty member in the classroom, but rather about the effectiveness of the collective faculty in facilitating student learning. We now return to the requirements for the Middle States Commission on Higher Education's Standard 14:

2. A documented, organized, and sustained assessment process to evaluate and improve student learning that meets the following criteria:
   - Systematic, sustained, and thorough use of *multiple* [my emphasis] qualitative and/or quantitative measures that
     ○ Maximize the use of existing data and information;
     ○ Clearly and purposefully relate to the goals they are assessing;
     ○ Are of sufficient quality that the results can be *used* with confidence to inform decisions;
     ○ Include direct evidence of student learning.
   - Clear, realistic guidelines and timetables that are supported by appropriate investment of institutional resources. (2006, 66–67)

Just as grades are inappropriate as a solitary measure for describing student learning, there is no single metric that fully describes cognitive gains. In assessing student learning, the Middle States Commission on Higher Education requires that institutions provide multiple pieces of evidence that clearly document the extent of student gains with respect to stated expected learning outcomes at the course, program, and institutional level. Various approaches to gathering these multiple measures will be discussed shortly.

The second requirement just noted is that student learning assessments must actually be used to inform decision making. Any regional or program accreditor will say that the problem is no longer one of getting institutions to engage in assessment of student learning; rather, the difficulty is in getting institutions to close the loop and actually use the data for institutional improvement. For example, the University of Delaware had a substantial grant in the mid-1990s to study the extent to which problem-based learning was more or less effective in overall student learning than the traditional lecture approach used in most courses. In problem-based learning, students work collaboratively in small groups, with the faculty member serving as a guide and resource rather than an information dispenser. The upshot of the research was that evidence garnered from assessment of student learning outcomes in several disciplines in the arts and sciences clearly demonstrated greater gains by students in problem-based learning classes than in traditional classes. Not surprisingly, problem-based learning became the pedagogy of choice in those disciplines. Consequently, when a new classroom building was constructed at the University of Delaware in 1995, the architecture of the building was modified to include multiple small-group work rooms to support the problem-based learning pedagogy. Assessment data clearly drove academic planning for the relevant disciplines, which in turn drove facilities planning at the institution.

In a similar vein, the Office of Residence Life at the University of Delaware sees its role as one of active partnership with Academic Affairs in supporting student learning. When the Faculty Senate adopted a new General Education Framework in 2000, Residence Life saw that as an opportunity for innovation. When new residence halls were constructed on the North Campus from 2004 through 2007, learning communities were structured in those residence halls, organized around the ten General Education skills (critical thinking, analytical reasoning, service learning, collaborative problem-solving, and so on) articulated by the Faculty Senate.

The final requirements under the Middle States Commission on Higher Education's Standard 14 are

3. Assessment results that provide sufficient, convincing evidence that students are achieving key institutional and program learning outcomes;

4. Evidence that student learning assessment is shared and discussed with appropriate constituents and is used to improve teaching and learning;

5. Documented use of student learning assessment information as part of institutional assessment. (2006, 67)

Requirements 3 and 5 are actually interrelated. Having the capacity to provide sufficient and convincing evidence that students are achieving institutional and programmatic learning goals is a fundamental reason why colleges and universities are in business. Absent that capacity, there is certainly reason to call the institution's accreditation into question. And if institutional effectiveness is defined as a college or university making optimal use of its human and fiscal resources to support the teaching/learning process, then calibration of the extent to which students are meeting institutional and programmatic learning objectives informs the institution with respect to the efficacy of its resource deployment.

Finally, Standard 14 requires that learning assessments be shared and used. Although the University of Delaware's design of a classroom building predicated on data from student learning assessments is a somewhat dramatic example of information sharing and use, smaller steps are equally important. Faculty colleagues sharing assessment data within a course to improve student outcomes in the laboratory or collaborative student activity in service-learning courses are not making multimillion-dollar decisions, but their actions can impact student learning as profoundly as the physical design of the facilities in which learning takes place.

As noted in Chapter One, there is great commonality in the accreditation requirements in all six regional accreditation bodies across the United States in terms of assessment of student learning, assessment of institutional effectiveness, and how much those assessments inform strategic planning. Consequently, although the foregoing examples of accreditation requirements

specifically cite the Middle States Commission on Higher Education policy, the generic issues related to measuring student learning easily translate into the specific requirements from the other
five regional accrediting bodies as well.

Strategies for Measuring Student Learning

In discussing strategies for assessing student learning outcomes, this
volume will take a from-thirty-thousand-foot view of the process and
discuss those strategies only in the broadest terms. The purpose of
this discussion is to give the reader a general sense of strategies for
gathering multiple measures in describing student learning. Those
interested in a more detailed discussion of strategies for assessing
student learning should consult two excellent resources: Palomba,
Banta, and Associates' *Assessment Essentials: Planning, Implementing,
Improving* (1999) and Suskie's *Assessing Student Learning: A Common
Sense Guide*, second edition (2009).

Exhibit 4.1 summarizes the major categories of strategies for
assessing student learning outcomes presently in use across the
United States. As the exhibit notes, no one strategy is sufficient by
itself to adequately measure student learning. The Middle States
Commission on Higher Education Accreditation Standard 14 (and
all other regional accrediting bodies) requires the provision of
multiple measures of student learning as evidence of student cognitive gains within a discipline or within an institution. Which of the
strategies shown in the following list to employ in assessing student
learning is also discipline-specific. There is no one-size-fits-all approach to measuring cognitive gains. One would certainly hope that
the strategies used to assess learning among students in a department of chemical engineering would be different than those used to
assess learning among students in a department of philosophy. An
undergraduate research laboratory experience might be an appropriate final project for the former, whereas a senior thesis might well
fit the latter. And in both cases, the final project should be
augmented by other measures including tests, class projects, and

so on. A brief review of each category of learning outcomes assessment strategies seems appropriate.

Strategies for Assessing Student Learning Outcomes

Note: No single strategy is sufficient, in and of itself, in describing student learning. Assessment of learning outcomes requires the use of multiple measures to provide adequate evidence of student cognitive gains.

1. Standardized tests

    General education or discipline-specific achievement tests

    Frequently used to evaluate skills related to professional licensure

2. Locally produced tests and test items

    May be used as stand-alone or embedded

3. Portfolios

    Collections of student work specimens over time

    May be the most effective assessment strategy for synthesizing student skills

    Very labor intensive and expensive in constructing appropriate evaluative rubrics

4. Final projects

    Demonstrable evidence that student has mastered integration of concepts across or within a discipline

    Examples include senior thesis, undergraduate research project, senior art show or music recital

5. Capstone experiences

    Culmination of study within a discipline; for example, student teaching, internship, cooperative educational experience, and so on

Source: Modified from a slide presentation developed by Jeffrey Seybert of Johnson County Community College in Overland Park, Kansas.

1. *Standardized Tests:* Discipline-specific standardized tests to measure demonstrable skills and competencies are an efficient tool for professional licensure. Exams such as the Praxis series of tests for teacher licensure and certification, the National Council Licensure Exam (NCLEX) for registered and practical nurses, and the Uniform CPA Exam for accountants have established track records of assessing skills appropriate to the specific professions they represent. Educational Testing Service (ETS) has a series of college-level achievement tests in disciplines such as biology, chemistry, English literature, and psychology that assess student mastery of concepts within those disciplines; these are frequently used as a factor in determining admission to graduate school. Where standardized testing encounters some measure of controversy is in the extent to which these tests accurately measure general education skills. With multiple companies producing multiple instruments, each with its own content and psychometric methodology, is there consistency across those instruments in precisely what is being measured within constructs such as "critical thinking," "integrative reasoning," and so on? That is not to say that such instruments have no value. But caution should be exercised in interpreting the results at any given institution, and extreme care should be exercised in benchmarking any standardized test general education assessment across institutions using different assessment instruments. At this writing, the National Association of State Universities and Land Grant Colleges (NASULGC; www.nasulgc.org) is overseeing research that is attempting to assess the extent to which three widely used commercial standardized tests—the Collegiate Learning Assessment (CLA), the Measure of Academic Proficiency and Progress (MAPP), and the Collegiate Assessment of Academic Proficiency (CAAP)—actually measure common general education skills. This research is being undertaken as part of a Fund for the Improvement of Postsecondary Education (FIPSE) grant awarded by the U.S. Department of Education to NASULGC, the American

Association of State Colleges and Universities (AASCU; www .aascu.org), and the Association of American Colleges and Universities (AACU; www.aacu.org) to explore facets of assessment of student learning. This is important research, and we encourage the reader to monitor its progress. The extent to which different standardized tests demonstrably measure the same dimensions of skills such as critical thinking or quantitative reasoning will help quell some of the concern that presently centers on the use of testing to measure general education. Clearly, in an area such as assessment of general education outcomes, institutions are well served by gathering multiple measures of student achievement and providing multiple pieces of evidence of student cognitive gains that describe student growth in general education skills.

2. *Locally Produced Tests and Test Items:* Long a staple in assessing the performance of individual students, locally produced tests and test items can be a highly effective tool in assessing the aggregate mastery of concepts by students within a discipline. If the institution can convince all of the sections of Physics 101 or English 110 to use a common test to measure student mastery, it will be easier to assess the extent to which different pedagogies or teaching strategies contribute to that mastery. And absent a common test, common test items embedded in different tests in different course sections provide a common reference for assessing those different pedagogies and teaching styles. The advantage to locally prepared tests and test items is that, so long as they are reliable and valid in actually measuring the skills or gains that they purport to assess, they are relatively inexpensive and efficient tools for measuring student learning success.

3. *Portfolios:* Portfolios—hard copy or electronic—are far and away the most effective means of assessing student growth and competencies in general education skills areas such as critical thinking, quantitative reasoning, and the ability to integrate and synthesize complex ideas and communicate them effectively.

Portfolios are collections of specimens of individual student work, gathered over time, and submitted to a panel of faculty who judge the work against a carefully developed rubric or rubrics of evaluative criteria. Both the faculty panel and rubrics are consistent over the period of evaluation. Although student portfolios are highly effective tools for assessing student learning, they are also very expensive to implement. Substantial faculty time is required both to develop the rubric(s) to be used in the evaluation and to actually assess the content of the portfolios. Institutions typically sample students in gathering portfolio content, as a means of containing those costs, as measured in faculty time. Another difficulty associated with portfolios is the capacity to concisely and succinctly communicate the evaluative criteria within the assessment rubric(s) and the results of the assessments. But those difficulties aside, portfolios are a highly effective assessment technique. It is also noteworthy that AACU, under the same FIPSE grant referenced in the earlier discussion on standardized tests, is conducting extensive research on the feasibility of designing "meta-rubrics" that would allow the comparison of student electronic portfolios across institutional boundaries. This research is enormously important, as it would enable cross-institutional assessment of certain basic student learning outcomes using actual student work, as opposed to standardized testing. At this writing, the research has not been concluded, and the reader is once again encouraged to monitor its progress.

4. *Final Projects:* Portfolios are extremely useful in measuring mastery of general education skills; final projects are equally useful in measuring student acquisition of general content and skills within a specific discipline. Fine arts disciplines have done this for years, with studio art majors expected to exhibit in their senior year and provide a written paper describing how their work conceptually and technically evolved. Music majors are often expected to do the same in senior recitals, and theater

majors in senior performances. Other fields have taken the cue; they may require senior theses addressing topics that require students to integrate and synthesize ideas and concepts from courses taken throughout their academic career in the discipline. Natural and physical sciences and engineering often require an undergraduate research project in the senior year that requires students to draw on both course content and laboratory skills acquired over time to scientifically test specific hypotheses.

5. *Capstone Experiences:* Most typically used in professional disciplines, capstone experiences require students to demonstrate acquired skills and concepts in an on-the-job setting. Student teachers and clinical nurses are obvious examples, as are cooperative education students doing internships in businesses and companies. Capstone experiences go a long way in addressing employer criticisms that institutions graduate students without requisite experience for employment. Within the capstone environment, students either perform at acceptable standards or they don't. Feedback from organizational mentors in capstone experiences is often invaluable in refreshing and revitalizing the discipline's curriculum.

A Word About Assessment in Graduate Education

Most of what is currently being written about assessing student learning outcomes is focused almost exclusively on undergraduate education. This is due in no small part to the fact that graduate education has, historically, structurally contained assessment strategies within the various disciplines. Master's-level students are generally required to write a thesis, complete a practicum experience, or both to demonstrate competency in the discipline. Before advancing to degree candidacy, doctoral students are usually required to perform successfully on a comprehensive examination in the discipline, drawing on course work taken up to that point. Once in candidacy, the student must defend a dissertation proposal and, ultimately, write and defend the dissertation study. It is relatively easy to look at these activities in the aggregate to determine graduate student mastery of expected learning outcomes within the discipline.

That said, graduate departments are not exempt from the necessity and requirement to have clearly stated outcomes at the course level that correlate with expected outcomes for master's and doctoral graduates in the discipline, which in turn tie to overall institutional outcomes expected of graduate students. The discipline- and institutional-level learning outcomes for graduate students will likely be different from those for undergraduates, focusing more on highly refined integrative and research skills. However, these expected graduate student learning outcomes must be spelled out alongside those for undergraduates in the departmental and institution-wide assessment plans.

Communicating the Results of Assessment of Student Learning

When developing strategies for communicating the results of assessments of student learning, first and foremost we must keep in mind that there are different audiences with different information needs. There are internal audiences—largely faculty and academic support personnel—who need the information as the basis for decision making directed at improving the teaching/learning process at the institution. And there are external audiences—primarily parents, legislators, and others who underwrite the cost of students' attendance at college—who seek evidence that students are learning sufficiently to justify the financial investment.

When considering internal audiences, the focus should be on reporting the results of *direct* measures of student learning. Knowing how students perform in the aggregate on structured examinations, written papers, class projects, laboratory exercises, and so on within a given course provides faculty with essential information on the extent to which stated learning outcomes are being realized. This information may then be used to shape decisions with respect to pedagogical delivery, course prerequisites, course sequencing, curriculum redesign, and so on. Student performance in portfolios and final projects helps define the extent to which both discipline-specific and general education learning outcomes are achieved. These assessments help to shape not only the institutional curriculum but also expected outcomes in academic and student support services for which the mission is to support and enhance the teaching/learning process. Effective institutions communicate internally through regular departmental meetings, institution-wide assessment forums, and institutional assessment websites. An example of such web-based communication is the University of Delaware's Office of Educational Assessment website, http://assessment.udel.edu/, which not only provides internal exchange of information but also directs users to best-practice websites at other colleges and universities. American University in Washington, D.C., has long been an example of best practice in learning outcomes assessment; their website, http://www.american.edu/academic.depts/provost/oir/assessment.html, is rich in resources. Brookdale Community College in New Jersey (http://www.brookdale.cc.nj.us/pages/388.asp) is a particularly good resource for information on assessing student learning outcomes in the two-year college sector. Readers interested in an international perspective on assessing student learning outcomes are directed to the website of London Metropolitan University (LMU), https://intranet.londonmet.ac.uk/. LMU is a comprehensive university, structured on the American model, that serves significant numbers of first-generation and nontraditional students. The institution was recently accredited by the Middle States Commission on Higher Education, and their approach to assessment, rooted in the traditions of the British Quality Assurance Agency, was cited as an example of best practice. Universidad Mayor, in Santiago, Chile (http://www.umayor.cl/um/), has also taken an innovative approach to assessing student learning outcomes. Their general education curriculum, *Curriculum Mayor*, has been cast in specific student skills that are measurable across the full range of disciplines at the institution, ranging from liberal arts to specific professional disciplines. Although their website is in Spanish, because Universidad Mayor is a candidate for accreditation with the Middle States Commission on Higher Education, all of its core documents related to assessing student learning outcomes have been translated to English, and can be accessed by writing to the Director of Academic Planning at the University address listed on the website.

Communication of assessment results to external audiences may be somewhat problematic if direct assessments are used. Few parents or legislators have the patience to internalize templates for rubrics that are used to assess electronic portfolios. They are unlikely to show in-depth interest in the contents of a senior thesis or the research papers produced as the result of undergraduate research experiences. At least at this time, external audiences appear to be more focused on *indirect* measures of student learning. The number of an institution's graduates passing licensure exams in respective disciplines is one such indirect measure generally accepted as evidence that the students have learned. Many institutions post data such as those in Table 4.1 to describe post-graduation outcomes for students as proxy evidence that they have acquired the necessary knowledge and skills to secure employment or move on to graduate school.

As noted in Chapter One, data of the sort displayed in Table 4.1 will be a component in the institutional data reporting template being developed by the NASULGC, AASCU, and AAC&U for the Voluntary System of Accountability (VSA). Other indirect measures of student learning to be included in the VSA template are aggregate student responses to selected items on the National Survey of Student Engagement (NSSE) and aggregate student scores on one of the three standardized tests: CLA, CAAP, or MAPP. Although transparency and disclosure with respect to student learning are imperative in interactions with external constituencies, the institution should take great care in selecting which measures to report. Licensure exam pass rates and post-graduation placement activity are tangible and fairly unambiguous measures that bear

Table 4-1 Employment and Educational Status of Baccalaureates by Curriculum Group, Class of 2006

Curriculum Group	Number in Class	Number of Respondents[1]		Full-Time Employment	Part-Time Employment	Pursuing Further Education	Still Seeking Employment
		n	%	%	%	%	%
Agriculture & Natural Resources	167	61	36.5	52.5	6.6	36.1	3.3
Arts & Sciences, Humanities	434	139	32.0	64.0	5.8	21.6	7.9
Social Sciences	884	292	33.0	55.8	5.5	29.1	7.2
Life & Health Sciences	150	54	36.0	33.3	5.6	50.0	7.4
Physical Sciences	234	84	35.9	59.5	4.8	29.8	4.8
Business & Economics	566	252	44.5	91.7	–	4.0	4.0
Engineering	206	127	61.7	80.3	–	18.1	1.6
Health Sciences	394	156	39.6	70.5	3.8	23.7	1.3
Human Services, Education & Public Policy	575	224	39.0	84.8	4.5	8.0	2.2
2006 University Total[2]	3,610	1,389	38.5	70.9	3.7	19.9	4.4

Note: Percentages may not total to 100.0 because of rounding.

[1]The 2006 Career Plans Survey represents survey respondents from the full baccalaureate graduating class.

[2]Eight (0.6%) of the 1,389 respondents indicated they are not seeking work. University total includes all curriculum groups.

some correlation to student learning over the collegiate career. If an institution opts to share data from the NSSE or some other indirect measure of student learning, it would be wise to provide context for exactly which variables are being measured in the instrument and how much control the institution has over those variables. Certainly a college or university wants to provide an intellectually rigorous environment in which students are challenged to read and write extensively, both in and outside of classes, to engage in collaborative learning activities with students and faculty, and to contribute to the quality of life on campus and in the larger societal context. That said, institutions have no direct control over the extent to which students take advantage of such opportunities, nor do they have control over how seriously and conscientiously students respond to such a data collection instrument. Quite frankly, instruments such as the NSSE are better used as gauges for internal academic planning to develop and enhance activities that support stated expected collegiate outcomes than as vehicles for external reporting of student learning experiences.

Similarly, the use of standardized test scores as measures of student achievement of general education skills is dicey, at best. Is the institution in a position to assure external constituents that the instrument is precisely measuring the skill(s) that it purports to, and can it assure those constituents that students have conscientiously approached a test that has absolutely no bearing on their progress toward a degree? Not likely, and this puts serious limitations on the information being conveyed. To counter this objection, a number of institutions are incorporating standardized tests of general education skills into the curriculum of specific courses leading to the receipt of a degree.

Indirect measures such as employer satisfaction surveys, success in graduate school, and alumni surveys that assess the ongoing relevance of the educational experience at an institution are useful assessments when coupled with other measures such as licensure pass rates and postgraduation placement. Colleges and universities must report credible measures of student success to those outside of the academy. But great care should be taken in selection of those measures and in providing appropriate context for what is being reported.

Summary

Measuring student learning in multiple meaningful and credible ways is essential to understanding the extent to which students are achieving formally stated expectations for the knowledge and skills to be acquired at the course, discipline, and institutional level. A systematic program of assessment of student learning provides the evidence base for curricular design and reform directed at optimizing teaching and learning on campus. It also provides a road map for deploying human and fiscal resources in a manner that enhances teaching and learning at the institution. Specific examples of this will be described in later chapters.

Student learning assessment also provides a vehicle for communicating information about student success to those outside of the institution. However, care must be exercised in choosing the information that is communicated and in the context in which that communication takes place. Information should reflect those measures of success over which the institution has some measure of control.

5

MAXIMIZING HUMAN AND FISCAL RESOURCES IN SUPPORT OF THE TEACHING/LEARNING PROCESS

As described in Chapter One, there is no shortage of frustration with the inability of the American higher education system to adequately explain how it operates. The National Commission on the Cost of Higher Education (1998) was highly critical of data that purported to explain how faculty spend their time, and the relationship of faculty activity to escalating tuition prices. The Spellings Commission (2006) chastised higher education officials for lack of transparency and accountability in discussing the relationship between the cost of a college education and demonstrable student learning outcomes. Highly effective institutions must develop metrics that address these concerns in a serious fashion. Chapter Four described the need to develop multiple, credible measures that describe student learning. This chapter will focus on measuring faculty productivity and instructional costs as the other two central components of transparency and accountability that are essential to addressing the central concerns of both the National Commission on the Cost of Higher Education and the Spellings Commission.

The higher education community in the United States does not have a particularly stellar record when it comes to describing faculty productivity and associated instructional costs. Faculty activity has generally been described in terms of the percentage of time spent in discrete categories of activity, such as teaching, research, service, and subcategories within those three general headings. Middaugh (2001) described in some detail strategies for reporting faculty activity in the National Study of Postsecondary Faculty (NSOPF, http://nces.ed.gov/surveys/nsopf/), a national data collection activity under the aegis of the National Center for Education Statistics that takes place every five years. A number of NSOPF tables examine allocation of faculty time that is analyzed in terms of the percentage of time spent in teaching activities, research activities, administrative activities, and other activities. Other tables measure variables such as average number of hours spent in the classroom, mean student contact hours, and average number of scholarly outputs, such as publications, presentations, exhibits, and patents. The University of California at Los Angeles's Higher Education Research Institute (HERI; http://www.gseis.ucla.edu/heri/facOverview.php) annually collects data through their Faculty Survey, which produces a rich tapestry of data that describe not only how faculty allocate their time (going beyond NSOPF and looking at campus functions such as academic advising and institutional committee work) but also the various teaching strategies they employ in the classroom, such as team teaching, problem-based learning, and cooperative education.

Although both NSOPF and the HERI Faculty Survey collect information of value to policymakers, it is not the sort of data needed to address the concerns of the two commissions cited earlier. NSOPF and HERI describe faculty activity primarily in terms of *inputs*. If faculty spend, on average, 60 percent of their time teaching, 30 percent in research, and 10 percent in service, so what? Parents, legislators, and others funding the cost of higher education want to know whether students can demonstrate measurable returns on the time faculty invest in teaching. To a lesser extent, there is pressure to demonstrate the extent to which faculty research and public service are contributing to the public good. Gone are the days of the 1960s, when Senator William Proxmire of Wisconsin periodically awarded his Golden Fleece Award to universities engaging in what he, and the general public for that matter, determined to be largely irrelevant research activity. Although no longer regularly held up to broad public ridicule, colleges and universities are expected to be able to make clear linkages between research and service activity and the general welfare of the public at large.

The question, then, is how does an institution begin to build credible evidence of teaching productivity and instructional cost containment that is both transparent and accessible to nonacademics? A second area of difficulty beyond the inputs issue with both the NSOPF and HERI data is that they largely describe faculty at the institutional level of aggregation, and where disaggregation occurs, it is into broad curricular areas such as fine arts, humanities, social sciences, natural and physical sciences, and so on. Any credible data related to instructional costs and productivity must be developed at the level of the academic department and discipline. Middaugh, Graham, and Shahid (2003) examined three data collection cycles from the Delaware Study of Instructional Costs and Productivity (a data-sharing consortium that will be discussed in Chapter Six) and found that over 80 percent of the variation in instructional costs across four-year institutions in the United States that participate in the Delaware Study is explained by the mix of disciplines that make up the academic curriculum at the institution. Upon reflection, we should not be surprised by this finding. Some disciplines, particularly in the physical sciences and engineering, are laboratory- and equipment-intensive and require smaller class sizes, whereas other disciplines, most notably in the humanities and social sciences, readily lend themselves to lecture format and, frequently, larger class sections. Yet other disciplines—particularly in the fine arts, clinical nursing, and teacher education—call for class sections that require some form of individualized instruction. And like it or not, not all four-year faculty are compensated equally. Engineering and business faculty command different salaries from philosophy and sociology faculty. There will be more discussion of cost drivers later in the next chapter. The important point here is that the academic department or discipline must be the lens for analyzing instructional costs and productivity.

Developing Appropriate Analytical Metrics

In thinking about assessing instructional productivity and costs as essential information for effectively managing human and fiscal resources in support of the teaching/learning process, we need to address this focal question: "Who is teaching what to whom, and at what cost?" Which faculty are teaching which courses, and what is the magnitude of the expenditures for the instructional function? Equally important, what are the outcomes of faculty activity? These are not trivial questions, and establishing appropriate metrics requires extended conversations among various campus constituencies to arrive at consensus on those metrics. Although there is no single best template or formula for engaging in such conversations, the experience at the University of Delaware may prove instructive.

In 1988, the University of Delaware was faced with a severe regional economic recession, reduced support in terms of state appropriation, and the need to bring a deficit budget into balance. The administration set out on a deliberate course of action to bring long-term budget stability to the institution that would minimize negative financial impact to the academic core of the University— that is, classroom instruction and academic support services. That said, it was nonetheless apparent that at some point academic units would have to engage in discussions about how to reallocate financial resources to best support institutional learning goals. The strategy for achieving long-term financial stability included the following components:

- Budget savings would be achieved, in part, through tighter position control with respect to hiring. During the budget rebalancing phase, as positions became vacant through resignations and retirements, the budget lines associated with those positions were eliminated.

- The University outsourced functions that were not critical to the institution's mission, but which were funded wholly or in large part by the institution's basic budget. These included functions such as dining services, the university bookstore, and pharmaceutical services in the student health center. To the greatest extent possible, in negotiating contracts with outsourcing partners, University employees became employees of the respective outsourcing partner.

• The University took advantage of technology to move from paper-intensive business practices, which required a substantial cadre of clerical employees to process paper forms, to a web-based environment that required virtually no paper forms and far fewer employees to oversee processing of web forms.

While these sorts of activities were resulting in significant reductions in administrative expense, an infrastructure was being created to examine academic expense, particularly as it related to teaching, with an eye toward building capacity for making decisions about resource reallocation, as it was clearly evident that there would be no substantial infusion of new money for the foreseeable future. The Office of Institutional Research and Planning at the University of Delaware was responsible for meeting with appropriate academic units to arrive at a mutually acceptable set of metrics that would describe instructional costs and productivity and provide a basis for making sound fiscal decisions. In developing what came to be known as "Budget Support Notebooks," the following guiding principles shaped the discussions among personnel from the Office of Institutional Research and Planning, academic deans, department chairs, and representatives from the Faculty Senate Planning and Budgeting Committee:

• Data will be used not to reward or penalize units, but rather as a tool of inquiry for determining whether substantial differences in variables reflecting either productivity or cost among appropriate comparator departments could be explained in terms of quality issues.

- Data from a single fiscal or academic year will never be used for resource allocation or reallocation decisions. The objective is to develop trend indicators; then reliable decisions could be made on the basis of long-term performance. Single-year data can be idiosyncratic, impacted by variables such as faculty sabbaticals, enrollment spikes, and extraordinary expenses in a given year as the result of factors such as professional accreditation activity.

- Only when a department or program displays exceptionally high cost and low productivity over time when viewed against appropriate comparator units, and those differences cannot be explained in terms of quality, does that unit become a candidate for resource reallocation. Similarly, when a clearly high-quality unit displays productivity and cost measures over time that, when compared with other units, suggest an inequity with respect to either human or fiscal resources, only then does that unit become a candidate for additional resource allocation.

- Data will be transparent. Any given academic unit not only will have access to their own productivity and cost measures, but also will have access to equivalent measures for all of the other academic units on campus. Resource allocation decisions can be effective only when affected units have a role in shaping the measures used in those decisions, have a clear understanding of the ground rules for those decisions, and understand how the decisions are being applied across the institution. This requires data transparency.

Based on these guidelines, the conversations resulted in the production of an annual snapshot of instructional productivity and costs for each academic unit at the University that encompasses the following elements:

- FTE Majors
- Degrees Granted
- Student Credit Hours Taught, by Level of Instruction

- Percent of Credit Hours Taught by Recurring Faculty
- Percent of Student Credit Hours Consumed by Non-Majors
- FTE Students Taught
- FTE Faculty
- Student Credit Hours Taught per FTE Faculty
- FTE Students Taught per FTE Faculty
- Direct Expenditures on Separately Budgeted Research and Service
- Direct Expense on Instruction
- Earned Income from Instruction

Although such a list may seem straightforward, the conversations among the metric architects focused on interpretation and use of the information derived from the data. Table 5.1 displays these metrics for a humanities department at the University of Delaware.

Table 5.1 shows a relatively small department in terms of majors and degrees granted—an exclusively undergraduate unit with about forty majors and twenty degrees awarded each year. If these were the only metrics considered, it would be tempting to close down this unit. However, when the number of student credit hours taught each term—usually well in excess of six thousand—is considered, it is evident that forty departmental majors are not the sole consumers of the department's teaching activity. Indeed, the percentage of those student credit hours consumed by non-majors consistently hovers around 97 percent, suggesting that students who rely on this humanities unit to satisfy general education requirements would be seriously disadvantaged by any decision to reallocate resources away from this unit. Moreover, the data show that eight out of ten student credit hours are delivered by recurring faculty, referred to in Table 5.1 as "Faculty on Appointment."

In examining the issue of productivity, the decision was made early on to consider the number of majors in a department; this is reflected as the first item in Table 5.1. However, majors are

Table 5-1   Budget Support Data, 2004–05 to 2006–07, College of Arts and Science, Department X

	A. Teaching Workload Data					
	Fall 2004	Fall 2005	Fall 2006	Spring 2005	Spring 2006	Spring 2007
FTE Majors						
Undergraduate	38	31	39	38	40	39
Graduate	0	0	0	0	0	0
Total	38	31	39	38	40	39
Degrees Granted						
Bachelor's	—	—	—	20	19	19
Master's	—	—	—	0	0	0
Doctorate	—	—	—	0	0	0
Total	—	—	—	20	19	19
Student Credit Hours						
Lower Division	6,246	5,472	5,448	4,518	6,156	5,478
Upper Division	726	638	869	1,159	951	966
Graduate	183	153	129	195	276	135
Total	7,155	6,263	6,446	5,872	7,383	6,579
% Credit Hours Taught by Faculty on Appointment	77%	81%	77%	82%	91%	82%
% Credit Hours Taught by Supplemental Faculty	23%	19%	23%	18%	9%	18%
% Credit Hours Consumed by Non-Majors	98%	97%	98%	96%	98%	97%
FTE Students Taught						
Lower Division	416	365	363	301	410	365
Upper Division	48	43	58	77	63	64
Graduate	20	17	14	22	31	15
Total	484	425	435	400	504	444

Table 5-1   (Continued)

A. Teaching Workload Data

	Fall 2004	Fall 2005	Fall 2006	Spring 2005	Spring 2006	Spring 2007
FTE Faculty						
Department Chair	1.0	1.0	1.0	1.0	1.0	1.0
Faculty on Appointment	15.0	16.0	15.0	15.0	15.0	15.0
Supplemental Faculty	1.5	1.0	1.3	1.0	0.8	1.5
Total	17.5	18.0	17.3	17.0	16.8	17.5
Workload Ratios						
Student Credit Hrs./ FTE Faculty	408.9	347.9	373.7	345.4	440.8	375.9
FTE Students Taught/FTE Faculty	27.7	23.6	25.2	23.5	30.1	25.4

B. Fiscal Data

	FY 2005 ($)	FY 2006 ($)	FY 2007 ($)
Research and Service			
Research Expenditures	0	5,151	499
Public Service Expenditures	0	0	0
Total Sponsored Research/Service	0	5,151	499
Sponsored Funds/FTE Faculty on Appointment	0	312	31
Cost of Instruction			
Direct Instructional Expenditures	1,068,946	1,141,927	1,144,585
Direct Expense/Student Credit Hour	81	84	88
Direct Expense/FTE Student Taught	1,198	1,229	1,301
Revenue Measures			
Earned Income from Instruction	3,960,208	4,366,720	4,311,275
Earned Income/Direct Instructional Expense	3.73	3.82	3.77

essentially a measure of input and do not reflect output from teaching activity. Consequently, it was decided to add "FTE Students Taught" to the list of metrics to reflect the number of full-time students generated from teaching. The operating assumption is common across institutional research offices nationally: the typical undergraduate at a four-year institution carries a term load of 15 credits (usually 18 at a community college), whereas a typical graduate student has a term load of 9 hours. Under the "Student Credit Hours" field in Table 5.1, if lower and upper division credit hours are divided by 15, and graduate credit hours are divided by 9, the resultant measure is an expression of full-time equivalents generated from teaching activity within a unit. When used in a ratio with FTE faculty, the twenty-five to thirty students taught per FTE faculty in this unit is a meaningful measure of workload. Unlike the more traditional student/faculty ratio used by many admissions guidebooks, which asks for total full-time students at the institution to be divided by total full-time faculty, FTE Students Taught per FTE Faculty in these metrics reflect teaching activity; the former is simply a function of head count and is not at all sensitive to differences among academic disciplines.

Marrying measures of teaching workload to fiscal measures required substantial conversation as these metrics were developed. Although the focus is on teaching productivity, many deans and department chairs were quick to point out that there are other important measures of departmental productivity, particularly in the areas of research and public service. It was important to develop a mechanism whereby, in instances in which teaching productivity is lower and instructional costs are higher for a unit within appropriate interdisciplinary comparisons, they could determine whether that could be attributed to the fact that faculty are engaged in other mission-related activities; that is, research and service. Separately budgeted research and service expenditures (generally attributable to externally funded contracts and grants or institutional matching funds) became the proxy for research and service activity; these are divided by recurring FTE faculty to arrive at research and service expenditures per faculty. Given the dearth of external funds for arts and humanities, the relatively low ratios in Table 5.1 are not surprising. (Yes, there are departments that have little or no access to external funds, but scholarship and service are expectations for promotion and tenure. This issue, and strategies for addressing it, will be discussed later in this book.)

Having identified a proxy for assessing research and service activity, the discussion then focused on instructional expense. How can the cost of instruction best be expressed in a manner that is both transparent and credible? It was decided that the measurement would focus on *direct instructional expense*, as opposed to attempting to developing a full cost model. As discussions progressed, it became apparent that if there are, say, fifty-four academic units at the University of Delaware, there are at least fifty-four different ways of calculating what are referred to as indirect costs; that is, administrative (admissions, registration, and so on) and other costs (facilities, utilities, and so on) associated with operating an academic department or program. On the other hand, the definition of what constitutes a direct expense for instruction or research or service is consistent not only across departments within an institution but also across departments among institutions. These definitions are consistent with those developed for the National Center for Education Statistics' Integrated Postsecondary Education Data System (IPEDS) and are found in Appendix B of this volume. Using the student credit hours taught and FTE students taught measures developed earlier, it is possible to calculate direct instructional expense per student credit hour and FTE student taught.

The next step was to calculate a measure that assessed the relationship between earned income from instruction and direct expense for instruction. Keep in mind that this is an analysis to support policy decisions, not an accounting exercise. The University of Delaware is a public institution with both Delaware resident and nonresident students who pay different tuition rates. In calculating earned income from instruction for this purpose, the concern is not to determine which students in a given class are from Newark,

Delaware, and which are from Newark, New Jersey, but rather to obtain a general estimate of revenue generated from teaching. Total tuition revenue at the University for a given fiscal year is divided by total student credit hours taught during the corresponding academic year to arrive at a "per credit hour unit measure of revenue." That per credit hour unit measure is then multiplied by the number of student credit hours taught in Part A of Table 5.1 to arrive at earned income from instruction for this particular unit. Earned income from instruction is then divided by direct instructional expense for that year to produce an income-to-expense ratio, which is useful for comparing the relationship between cost and productivity across departments.

Table 5.2 shows comparable metrics for an entirely different type of department at the University.

This is an exclusively graduate program in the physical sciences. Its workload ratios are significantly lower than the humanities unit, and its cost per credit hour and FTE student taught are much higher. Its income-to-expense ratio is but a fraction of that for the humanities unit. Although physical science units and humanities units should not be compared, if the metrics just cited were all that factored into the decision, even this inappropriate comparison would suggest that the physical sciences unit be targeted for reduction or elimination. However, examination of research and service expenditures per FTE faculty shows that each faculty member accounts for a quarter million dollars in external funds. And when one considers how graduate students in the physical sciences are taught, it can't be measured solely in terms of credit hours or FTE students taught per faculty. It must also be assessed in terms of the interaction between faculty and graduate research assistants in the laboratory. And at $250,000 in contracts and grants per recurring faculty, clearly research is taking place within this unit.

These budget support metrics not only provided academic units at the University of Delaware with an empirical basis for thinking about resource allocation and reallocation decisions but also provided a basis for illustrating how each respective unit contributes in

Table 5-2   Budget Support Data, 2004–05 to 2006–07, Graduate Program in Physical Sciences

A. Teaching Workload Data

	Fall 2004	Fall 2005	Fall 2006	Spring 2005	Spring 2006	Spring 2007
FTE Majors						
Undergraduate	0	0	0	0	0	0
Graduate	75	74	94	72	73	87
Total	75	74	94	72	73	87
Degrees Granted						
Bachelor's	~~~~	~~~~	~~~~	0	0	0
Master's	~~~~	~~~~	~~~~	15	14	15
Doctorate	~~~~	~~~~	~~~~	9	7	9
Total	~~~~	~~~~	~~~~	24	21	24
Student Credit Hours						
Lower Division	210	156	216	0	0	0
Upper Division	10	43	46	70	12	31
Graduate	848	668	759	740	718	696
Total	1,068	867	1,021	810	730	727
% Credit Hours Taught by Faculty on Appointment	96%	96%	95%	95%	95%	92%
% Credit Hours Taught by Supplemental Faculty	4%	4%	5%	5%	5%	8%
% Credit Hours Consumed by Non-Majors	3%	2%	3%	0%	0%	0%
FTE Students Taught						
Lower Division	14	10	14	0	0	0
Upper Division	1	3	3	5	1	2
Graduate	94	74	84	82	80	77
Total	109	87	101	87	81	79
FTE Faculty						
Department Chair	0.0	0.0	0.0	0.0	0.0	0.0

(continued)

Table 5-2 (Continued)

A. Teaching Workload Data

	Fall 2004	Fall 2005	Fall 2006	Spring 2005	Spring 2006	Spring 2007
Faculty on Appointment	31.0	30.8	28.8	31.0	29.8	27.8
Supplemental Faculty	0.3	0.3	0.3	0.5	0.3	0.3
Total	31.3	31.1	29.1	31.5	30.1	28.1
Workload Ratios						
Student Credit Hours/ FTE Faculty	34.1	27.9	35.0	25.7	24.2	25.9
FTE Students Taught/ FTE Faculty	3.5	2.8	3.5	2.8	2.7	2.8

B. Fiscal Data

	FY 2005 ($)	FY 2006 ($)	FY 2007 ($)
Research and Service			
Research Expenditures	7,205,881	6,170,077	6,829,638
Public Service Expenditures	959,191	1,078,595	1,085,352
Total Sponsored Research/Service	8,165,072	7,248,672	7,914,990
Sponsored Funds/FTE Faculty on Appointment	263,389	239,072	279,484
Cost of Instruction			
Direct Instructional Expenditures	1,627,935	1,760,309	2,329,922
Direct Expense/Student Credit Hour	867	1,102	1,333
Direct Expense/FTE Student Taught	8,316	10,475	12,858
Revenue Measures			
Earned Income from Instruction	570,912	511,040	578,588
Earned Income/Direct Instructional Expense	0.35	0.29	0.25

one way or another to the institution's mission of teaching, research, and service. Clearly, the humanities unit in Table 5.1 contributes significantly to the teaching component; the physical sciences unit in Table 5.2 contributes significantly to the research mission. The departments in the College of Agriculture and Natural Sciences and in the School of Urban Affairs and Public Policy have data that demonstrate substantial contributions to the public service component of the institutional mission. The fact that the data for each academic unit is shared with all of the others across the institution helped transform the University from a loose confederation of fifty-four fiefdoms operating independently of each other into a *university*: one institution with a common mission to which each unit contributes. Having common metrics that are broadly understood and accepted has enabled the institution to make difficult decisions in lean years and better decisions in more prosperous years—both highly sought-after characteristics when assessing institutional effectiveness.

It is important to underscore the notion that these metrics are not intended for formula-driven resource allocation decisions. As noted earlier, budget support data are intended to serve as tools of inquiry into why a given department is similar to or different from appropriate peer units. It is totally plausible that an academic department might have higher costs and lower teaching productivity than other comparable units as the result of intentionally smaller classes intended to result in superior educational outcomes. However, if a unit is going to make that case, it is important to have multiple measures of student learning as described in Chapter Four. Similarly, particularly in university settings, a unit might argue that reduced teaching activity will result in increased research or service activity. Again, if that case is made, the results over time had better demonstrate the desired outcome. Just such an example will be found in a discussion of data benchmarking in Chapter Six.

When building budget support metrics such as those seen in the Budget Support Notebooks in Tables 5.1 and 5.2, it is important to develop tools for sharing and verifying data in preliminary fashion before actually incorporating the information into the Budget Support Notebook for use in resource allocation and reallocation decisions. Budget support metrics are designed to address our seminal question, "Who is teaching what to whom, and at what cost?" The "who is teaching what to whom" component can be addressed through a process of course verification wherein leaders—deans, department chairs, unit heads—verify course rosters to determine essential information related to teaching assignments. Consider the prototypic verification form in Table 5.3.

For each faculty member in the department, the verification form specifies the course(s) for which he or she is instructor of record. Other information relevant to the specific budget support data needs of an institution should also be included. In the prototype in Table 5.3, this includes the credit value of the course, the home department (that is, salary source) of the instructor, percent load (100 percent indicates sole instructor, 50 percent indicates two team teachers, 33 percent indicates three team teachers, and so on) as well as basic student enrollment information.

The verification form allows for clarification of critical elements in the budget support metrics. Home department of the instructor is particularly important, as budget support analysis should occur through what is referred to as an "origin of instructor" lens. Suppose Mary Smith is a full professor budgeted to the sociology department, and this particular term her administered teaching load includes a section of SOC 201, but as part of an inter-departmental cooperative arrangement she is also teaching a section in the anthropology department, ANTH 302. Because her salary is funded entirely by the sociology department, the workload associated with the anthropology section is credited to sociology. Were this not the case, it is safe to surmise that interdisciplinary and interdepartmental teaching at most institutions would virtually cease.

Accuracy in the count of sections taught is also enhanced through this course verification procedure. It is common practice at larger, more complex institutions to cross-list and dual-list courses. For example, in Table 5.3 William Davis is teaching SOC 311. Students in Cultural Studies can also register for that course under their departmental call letters; in this case, CSC 311. But it is still one section, taught and paid for by the sociology

Table 5-3 Departmental Workload Verification Data

Name	Rank/Course(s)	# Organized Sections	Tenure/ Credits	Home Dept./ Course Type	% Load	Students Enrolled	Credits	Teaching Credits
Thomas Jones	Chairperson		Tenured	Sociology				
	SOC 454	1	3 Hrs.	Lecture	100	9	27	3
	SOC 964	0	3–12 Hrs.	Supv. Study	100	0	3	1
					Total	9	30	4
Mary Smith	Professor		Tenured	Sociology				
	SOC 201	1	3	Lecture	100	246	738	3
	ANTH 302	1	3	Lecture	100	100	300	3
					Total	346	1038	6
William Davis	Professor		Tenured	Sociology				
	CSC 311 Cross Listed with SOC 311	1	3 Hrs.	Lecture	100	8	24	
	SOC 311	1	3 Hrs.	Lecture	100	38	114	3

(continued)

Table 5-3 (Continued)

Name	Rank/Course(s)	# Organized Sections	Tenure/ Credits	Home Dept./ Course Type	% Load	Students		Teaching Credits
						Enrolled	Credits	
	Cross Listed with *CSC 311*							
	SOC 327	1	3 Hrs.	Lecture	100	13	39	3
	SOC 366	0	1–3 Hrs.	Supv. Study	100	1	1	1
	SOC 866	0	1–6 Hrs.	Supv. Study	100	1	3	1
Pauline Lee	Associate Professor	Tenured	Sociology					
	PSY667	1	1 Hr.	Lecture	100	3	3	
	Cross Listed with *SOC 667*							
	SOC 341	1	3 Hrs.	Lecture	100	37	111	3
	SOC 467	1	3 Hrs.	Lecture	100	23	69	3
	SOC 667	1	1 Hr.	Lecture	100	5	5	1
	Cross Listed with *PSY 667*				Total	68	188	7

Roger Brown	Tenure Track		Sociology			
Assistant Professor						
SOC 467	1	3 Hrs.	Lecture	100	7	21	3
400 Level Meets with 600 Level						
SOC 667	1	3 Hrs.	Lecture	100	1	3	
600 Level Meets with 400 Level						
SOC 213	1	3 Hrs.	Lecture	100	77	231	3
Cross Listed with WOMS 213						
WOMS 213	1	3 Hrs.	Lecture	100	21	63	
Cross Listed with SOC 213						
			Total	106	318	6

department, with that unit getting the entire credit for workload. Dual listing frequently occurs at institutions with graduate programs. In Table 5.3, Roger Brown is teaching a course that upper division students—typically seniors—can register for as SOC 467, while entering graduate students can register for it as SOC 667. It still is one course and should not be double counted.

When institutional leaders realize that course verification underpins data that will be used in resource allocation decisions, the verification process is taken seriously. Prior to the 1987 introduction of this process at the University of Delaware as a component of budget support metrics, the single most productive faculty member on that campus was that itinerant creature who frequently shows up as instructor of record on many campuses—"Dr. Staff." Since implementation of a course-based set of budget support metrics at the University of Delaware, Dr. Staff now teaches seven to ten course sections per term out of a total approaching twenty thousand. Those Dr. Staff sections are typically credit-by-examination courses, for whom such an instructor designation is perfectly appropriate. Where data errors have consequences, care is taken to ensure that information is correct—a characteristic of institutional effectiveness.

"At what cost" does instruction occur? Table 5.1 showed a total direct instructional expense of $1,144,585 in FY 2007 for the humanities department under examination. Where did that figure come from? At every college or university subscribing to generally accepted accounting principles, every budget transaction—whether the expenditure be for a box of paper clips or for a desktop computer—contains an object code and a function code. The object code indicates what the funds are being spent on—salaries, benefits, support costs including travel, supplies and expense, etc. The function code indicates the purpose of the expenditure—instruction, department research, separately budgeted research and service, etc. Table 5.4 provides the dean or unit head with a detailed summary of how that $1,144,585 in the humanities department is broken out within the instructional function. Table 5.4 is nothing

Table 5-4 Departmental Expenditures, by Object and by Function: Fiscal Year 2007, Undergraduate Department in Humanities

	Instruction (01–08)	Departmental Re- search (09)	Org. Activity, Educ. Depts. (10)	Research (21–39)	Public Service (41–43)	Academic Support (51–56)
Expenditures						
Salaries						
Professionals	27,570	0	0	0	0	0
Faculty						
Full-Time (Including Department Chair)	993,612	0	0	0	0	0
Part-Time (Including Overload)	23,985	0	0	0	0	0
Graduate Students	0	0	0	0	0	0
Postdoctoral Fellows	0	0	0	0	0	0
Tuition/Scholarship	0	0	0	0	0	0
Salaried/Hourly Staff	59,601	0	0	0	0	0
Fringe Benefits	0	0	0	0	0	0
Subtotal	1,104,768	0	0	0	0	0
Support						

Table 5-4 (Continued)

	Instruction (01–08)	Departmental Research (09)	Org. Activity, Educ. Depts. (10)	Research (21–39)	Public Service (41–43)	Academic Support (51–56)
Miscellaneous Wages	1,884	0	0	499	0	0
Travel	12,275	6,510	0	0	0	0
Supplies and Expenses	10,496	2,925	0	0	0	0
Occupancy and Maintenance	1,270	0	0	0	0	0
Equipment	0	0	0	0	0	0
Other Expenses	13,932	230	0	0	0	0
Credits and Transfers	0	0	0	0	0	0
Subtotal	39,817	9,665	0	499	0	0
Total Expenditures	1,144,585	9,665	0	499	0	0

more than a cross-tabulation of the departments expenditures, by object and by function, from the institution's accounting file for a given fiscal year. But it provides unit managers with appropriate detail as to how their expenditures are categorized in that fiscal year. And where the data might be challenged, it is possible to drill down to the single-transaction level. Again, knowing how funds are being expended, and for what purpose, is characteristic of an effective institution.

The budget support data templates just described have been shared over the past two decades with institutions across the United States; they are a fairly common approach to looking at teaching productivity and instructional costs at both four-year and two-year institutions. The policy questions may differ by institution, but the analytical approaches have common threads. Two-year institutions will typically be less focused on cost differences between the disciplines, as the compensation structure for faculty at most community colleges is more uniform across those disciplines— depending more on faculty rank, length of service, and highest earned degree, and less on market-driven salary pressures. On the other hand, community colleges focus more on the reliance on part-time faculty for instruction and the use of faculty for precollege or remedial instruction. Whatever the general concern, the aforementioned budget support metrics provide an analytical framework for delving into policy questions.

Extending the Budget Support Metrics

As useful as it is to be able to compare instructional productivity and cost among appropriate comparator departments within an institution, institutional effectiveness is more powerfully assessed when external benchmarks are available. Metrics such as student credit hours taught per FTE faculty and direct instructional expense per student credit hour taught within a given department are particularly useful when they can be compared with the same measures in departments that are actual peers and departments at institutions to which the focal college or university aspires. In the opening section of this chapter, we referred to the Delaware Study of Instructional Costs and Productivity as a data-sharing consortium that systematically collects detailed information on faculty teaching loads, instructional costs, and externally funded scholarship, all at the academic discipline level of analysis. Institutions that have developed budget support metrics such as those just discussed are in a position to use Delaware Study benchmarks to further illuminate and analyze those metrics. The next chapter provides a detailed discussion of the Delaware Study.

6

A COMPARATIVE CONTEXT FOR EXAMINING DATA ON TEACHING LOADS AND INSTRUCTIONAL COSTS

When David Roselle assumed the presidency of the University of Delaware in 1991, he was immediately confronted with the regional economic downturn and institutional budget deficit described in the previous chapter. He found the Budget Support Notebooks outlined in Chapter Five to be highly useful tools in reallocating resources within the University. But the central question that emerged in his mind was how University of Delaware measures compared with those at other institutions. He asked the Office of Institutional Research and Planning to attempt to collect comparable data from other institutions; out of that request, the Delaware Study of Instructional Costs and Productivity was born.

The initial Delaware Study data collection took place in 1992. Successive grants to the University of Delaware from the Teachers Insurance and Annuity Association-College Retirement Equities Fund (TIAA-CREF) in 1995 and the Fund for the Improvement of Postsecondary Education (FIPSE) from 1996 through 1999 underwrote the cost of annually bringing together a national panel of experts in measuring faculty teaching productivity and instructional costs. This panel of experts helped to develop and shape the data collection protocols used in the Delaware Study. The Delaware Study is now broadly acknowledged as *the* state-of-the-art data collection tool for measuring teaching productivity, instructional costs, and externally funded scholarship at the academic discipline level of analysis.

The Delaware Study of Instructional Costs and Productivity has had nearly six hundred participating four-year institutions since its inception, ranging from complex research universities to baccalaureate colleges. A comprehensive description of the Delaware Study can be found at www.udel.edu/ir/cost. Over the years, the University of Delaware was urged to expand the data collection to include two-year institutions. Due to personnel resource constraints and, more important, the fundamental differences in disciplinary instructional and cost structures between two- and four-year institutions, it did not make sense for the University of Delaware to take on this task. However, the project evaluator for the FIPSE grant that supported the Delaware Study from 1996 to 1999 was the director of Institutional Research and Assessment at Johnson County Community College in Kansas. He successfully applied for a FIPSE grant to underwrite a two-year college version of the Delaware Study, for which the director of the Delaware Study served as project evaluator. For readers from two-year institutions interested in a comparable benchmarking capability, the Kansas Study of Instructional Costs and Productivity offers analytical capability parallel to the Delaware Study, but within the context of two-year college operations. Their web address is http://www.kansasstudy.org/. For purposes of discussion in this volume, the focus will be on the Delaware Study instrumentation and analysis. However, these discussions are equally applicable to two-year institutions within the Kansas Study context.

Figure 6.1 displays the data collection form for the Delaware Study. As noted, this data collection form was developed and refined over a period of years by a Delaware Study Advisory Committee of experts from across the United States who specialize in measuring faculty workloads and instructional costs. The Advisory Committee met several times each year. The data collection form went through a number of iterations and was systematically vetted through Delaware Study participating institutions to ensure consistency in what is being measured. The resulting data collection form has provided stability and consistency in the national benchmarks that are generated from it. Each of the Delaware Study

Institution:

Department/Discipline:

Associated CIP Identifier:

Please indicate the average number of degrees awarded in this discipline at each degree level over the three year period from 2003-04 through 2006-07.

Bachelor's:
Master's :
Doctorate:
Professional:

Place an 'X' in the box below if this discipline is non-degree granting.

Place an "X" in the box below that describes your academic calendar

Semester
Quarter

A. INSTRUCTIONAL COURSELOAD: FALL SEMESTER, 2006

Please complete the following matrix, displaying student credit hours and organized class sections taught, by type of faculty, and by level of instruction. Be sure to consult definitions before proceeding. Do not input data in shaded cells except for those mentioned in the important note below that pertains to (G) and (J).

Faculty				Student Credit Hours								Organized Class Sections				
Classification	FTE Faculty (A) Total	(B) Separately Budgeted	(C) Instructional	(D) Lower Div. OC*	(E) Upper Div. OC*	(F) Undergrad Indiv. Instruct.	(G) Total Undergrad SCH	(H) Grad OC*	(I) Graduate Indiv. Instruct.	(J) Total Graduate SCH	(K) Total Student Credit Hours	(L) Lab/Disc/Rec. Sections	Other Section Types (Lecture, Seminar, etc.) (M) Lower Div.	(N) Upper Div.	(O) Graduate	(P) Total
Regular faculty: -Tenured/Tenure Eligible																
- Other Regular Faculty																
Supplemental Faculty		NA														
Teaching Assistants: - Credit Bearing Courses		NA														
- Non-Credit Bearing Activity		NA		NA	NA	NA	NA	NA	NA	NA	NA					
TOTAL																

In the box to the right, indicate the number of Graduate Individualized Instruction Student Credit Hours from the Total that are devote to supervised doctoral dissertation.

B. COST DATA: ACADEMIC AND FISCAL YEAR 2006-07

1. In the boxes below, enter the total number of student credit hours that were generated during Academic Year 2006-07 during terms that were supported by the department's instructional budget. (NOTE: Semester calendar institutions will typically report fall and spring student credit hours; quarter calendar institutions will usually report fall, winter, and spring student credit hours.)

A. Undergraduate
B. Graduate

2. In the boxes below, enter total ***direct*** expenditures for instruction in FY 2006-07

A. Salaries — Are the benefits included in the number reported for salaries (Y/N)?
B. Benefits — If the dollar value is not available, what percent of salary do benefits constitute at your institution?
C. Other than personnel expenditures.
D. Total

3. In the box below, enter total ***direct*** expenditures for separately budgeted research activity in FY 2006-07

4. In the box below, enter total ***direct*** expenditures for separately budgeted public service activity in FY 2006-07

Figure 6.1 2007-08 Delaware Study of Instructional Cost and Productivity

benchmarks for teaching loads, instructional costs, and externally funded scholarship represent what are termed "refined means." That is, for any given data element, the responses from all institutions submitting information for that element are averaged to arrive at an initial mean. Then those responses are examined to isolate those that are more than two standard deviations above or below that initial mean. These are then treated as outliers and are excluded from any further calculation. The remaining values are again averaged to arrive at a refined mean, free of undue influence from extreme data points.

In the data collection form, academic disciplines are categorized and compared based on the Classification of Instructional Programs

(CIP) code assigned by the institution from the National Center for Education Statistics CIP Taxonomy. Part A of the data collection form focuses on student credit hours taught and organized class sections met by level of instruction during the fall term of the respective academic year by each of four categories of faculty; that is, tenured or tenure-eligible, other regular faculty, supplemental faculty, and graduate teaching assistants. This disaggregation by faculty category enables institutions to monitor the volume of teaching done by each of the faculty categories in comparison with that at other like institutions. This is particularly important in responding to external charges that undergraduate students— particularly freshmen and sophomores—are rarely taught by tenured and tenure-eligible faculty. It also enables institutions to track the volume of teaching done by "other regular faculty." This category of faculty is the fastest-growing group within American higher education today. These are individuals who typically are hired into nontenurable lines with the expectation that they will do nothing but teach. These faculty are not expected to engage in scholarship or institutional service; the sole function is instruction. Ostensibly, the growth in number in this category of faculty frees tenured and tenure-eligible faculty to focus on research and other forms of scholarship. Having an accurate sense of "who is teaching what to whom" will prove critical during this period of change and transition with American higher education.

Part B of the data collection form requires fiscal information comparable to that seen earlier in the budget support metrics. Complete definitions are found in Appendix B. These fiscal measures are then married to credit hour data to develop measures of direct expense per student credit hour taught and per FTE student taught that are comparable across institutions. Each cell or data element on the data collection form is benchmarked and reported back to participating institutions in three separate reports:

- Carnegie Institutional Classification
- Highest Degree Offered

- Relative Emphasis on Undergraduate Versus Graduate Instruction

To illustrate how each of the three reports is used, consider the case of the University of Delaware. That institution is classified as Research University—Very High Activity in the 2005 Carnegie Institutional Taxonomy. In doing the first cut at interinstitutional benchmarking of Delaware Study data, University of Delaware disciplines are compared with the national benchmarks for Research University—Very High Activity institutions participating in the Delaware Study in any given year. However, the philosophy and anthropology departments at the University of Delaware confer only the baccalaureate degree, and comparing them with other research university departments with extensive graduate programs would be misleading in terms of both credit hour production and overall instructional expense. Hence the Highest Degree Offered report is used to compare philosophy and anthropology with other departments offering only the baccalaureate. The Department of Chemical Engineering at the University of Delaware offers both undergraduate and graduate degrees, but the focus of instruction is at the graduate—primarily doctoral—level of instruction. Other research universities participating in the Delaware Study have chemical engineering departments that focus primarily on training undergraduates. In this instance, the third report, which arrays benchmark data in quintiles based on the volume of undergraduate versus graduate student credit hour production, enables appropriate comparisons for disciplines such as chemical engineering.

Delaware Study data enable institutions to make important policy decisions with respect to effective deployment of human and fiscal resources in support of an institution's mission. Consider the following example of Delaware Study data usage in a science department at the University of Delaware.

Figure 6.2 shows the standard workload/cost charts used to track productivity among tenured and tenure-eligible faculty in academic departments at the University of Delaware. The charts

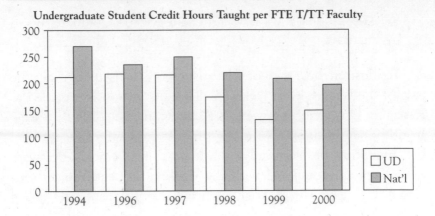

Undergraduate Student Credit Hours Taught per FTE T/TT Faculty

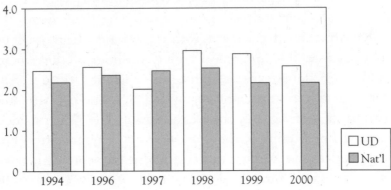

Total Class Sections Taught per FTE/TT Faculty

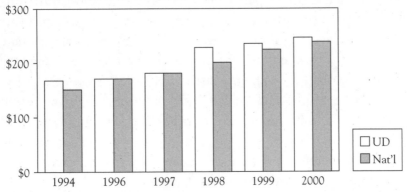

Direct Instructional Expenditures per Student Credit Hour

Figure 6.2 University of Delaware Academic Benchmarking: Science Department

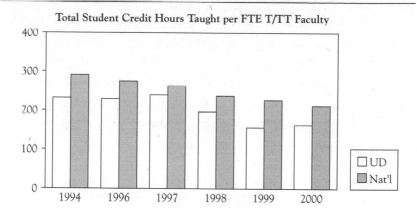

Total Student Credit Hours Taught per FTE T/TT Faculty

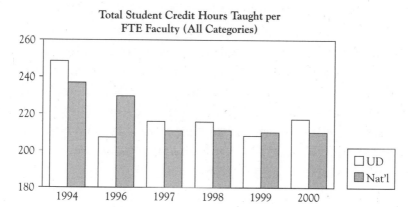

Total Student Credit Hours Taught per FTE Faculty (All Categories)

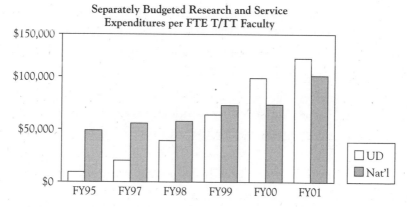

Separately Budgeted Research and Service Expenditures per FTE T/TT Faculty

Note: T = Tenured; TT = Tenure Track.

could be replicated for the other three faculty categories in the Delaware Study—recurring nontenurable faculty, supplemental faculty, and graduate teaching assistants. However, the focus on tenured and tenure-eligible faculty is understandable—these faculty are fixed costs; once tenure is granted, these faculty are with the institution until they retire or resign. And since 85 to 90 percent of direct instructional expense is accounted for by salaries, it is fair to measure the return on investment.

In the instance of the science department in Figure 6.2, the first two charts show that University of Delaware faculty productivity, measured in terms of undergraduate student credits hours taught and total student credit hours taught per FTE tenured and tenure track faculty, compares favorably in 1994 and 1996 to the national benchmark for research universities participating in the Delaware Study. However, the last chart, examining separately budgeted research activity (usually externally funded contracts and grants), shows the University lagging far behind the national benchmark in 1995 and 1997. In 1995, the University was offered the opportunity to participate in a technological consortium designed to attract scientific grants to the State of Delaware. However, to be effective in that consortium, the science department, as shown in Figure 6.2, would have to ramp up the level of grant activity. The chair of the department in question indicated a commitment to increased research activity, but to be successful, tenured and tenure-eligible faculty would require reduced teaching loads so they could prepare grant proposals and carry out the research, once funded. Consequently, the measures for student credit hours taught by this faculty category clearly decline from 1997 through 2000 in Figure 6.2. This is an intentional, planned decline, aiming to achieve the desired outcome with respect to research productivity. And the final chart in Figure 6.2 shows precisely the sort of desired outcome that was hoped for in years 1997 through 2000. This is a classic example of how Delaware Study benchmark data can be used to achieve greater institutional effectiveness. The data are used not to reward or penalize, but as a tool of inquiry to demonstrate where the institution is at a given point with respect to a particular issue or variable, and to guide policy on how to move forward. In the instance shown in Figure 6.2, the issue was to reduce teaching loads to achieve greater research productivity.

What happened to the student credit hours that were not being taught as the result of workload reductions among tenured and tenure-eligible faculty? The University saw the commitment to increased research activity among tenured and tenure-eligible faculty as a permanent situation. How then to replace those faculty? The University opted for a solution that is seeing increasing favor throughout the United States. Rather than hire new tenure-eligible faculty, the institution opted to hire faculty who would be placed on a recurring contract but for whom tenure would never be an outcome. These are the "Other Regular Faculty" on the Delaware Study Data Collection Form in Figure 6.1. As noted earlier, these faculty are hired strictly to teach; there is no expectation of scholarship or institutional service. Although tenured and tenure-eligible faculty typically teach two courses per term, a four-course load is not uncommon for these recurring teaching faculty. With this two-tiered faculty designation, the institution is maximizing its human resources with respect to both teaching and research functions.

Extending the Discussion of Costs

In the opening section of Chapter Five, mention was made of the 2003 study done by the author and his colleagues at the University of Delaware for the National Center for Education Statistics, using three cycles of data from the Delaware Study of Instructional Costs and Productivity (Middaugh, Graham, and Shahid, 2003). The study was part of a comprehensive response from NCES to a congressional call for an examination of factors that drive increases in tuition and instructional costs. The University of Delaware piece was titled *A Study of Higher Education Instructional Expenditures: The Delaware Study of Instructional Costs and Productivity*, and the analysis found that over 80 percent of the variation in direct instructional expense at four-year institutions in the United States can be explained by the disciplinary mix that forms the curriculum at a college or university. To illustrate why this is so, consider the disciplines in Figure 6.3—chemistry, English, foreign languages, mechanical engineering, and sociology. These disciplines are found at most four-year institutions, with the possible exception of mechanical engineering, which is more typically found at institutions with graduate instruction. Figure 6.3 looks at direct expense per student credit hour taught, by Carnegie institutional type within discipline.

Although there is some variation in each discipline, the spread from highest value to lowest value is fairly narrow—an $83 difference in chemistry, $28 in English, $71 in foreign languages, $63 in mechanical engineering, and $38 in sociology. On the other hand, when the analysis is refocused to look at direct expense per student credit hour taught, by discipline within each respective Carnegie

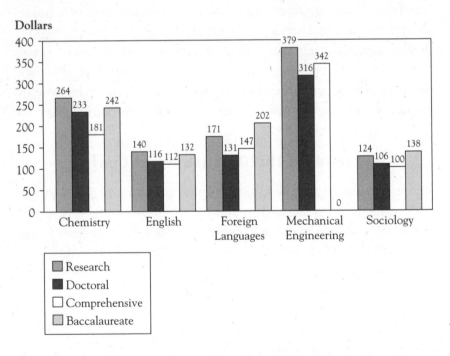

Figure 6.3 Direct Expense per Student Credit Hour Taught: Institution Type Within Discipline, Academic Year 2001

institutional type, the differences—as displayed in Figure 6.4—are striking and stunning.

At research universities, the spread between the highest-cost discipline, mechanical engineering, and the lowest-cost discipline, English, was $239 in academic year 2001. The spread between the most costly and least costly discipline at doctoral universities was $210; it was $242 at comprehensive institutions and $110 at baccalaureate colleges. Upon reflection, these disciplinary differences should not come as a major surprise. Faculty salaries constitute about 85 to 90 percent of direct instructional expense in a given academic discipline. In fall 2007, the average entry-level salary for newly minted Ph.D. assistant professors in mechanical engineering at largely public institutions across the United States participating

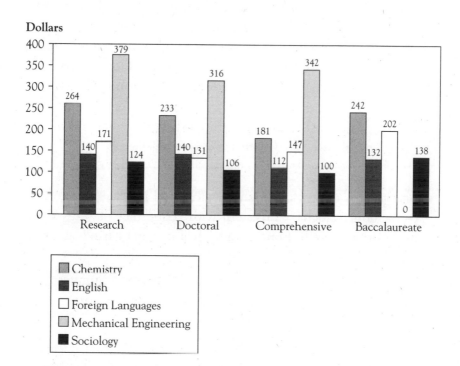

Figure 6.4 Direct Expense per Student Credit Hour Taught: Discipline Within Institution Type, Academic Year 2001

in the Oklahoma Salary Study was $77,450; in chemistry it was $62,230; in sociology, $59,230; in foreign languages, $53,000; and in sociology, $52,190. Among disciplines not analyzed in the foregoing comparisons, new assistant professors in finance had an average entry salary of $134,435; in business administration this was $113,320, and in economics, $85,270. Similar disciplinary differences are found in the College and University Professional Association for Human Resources (CUPA-HR) 2007–08 National Faculty Salary Survey for Four Year Institutions, which includes both public and private colleges and universities. (*Note:* The foregoing discussion of salary differentials, by discipline, underlines one of the fundamental differences between four-year and two-year colleges in analytical approaches to examining instructional costs. Such disciplinary differences are not seen at two-year institutions, where compensation is administered on uniform salary ladders that are a function of academic rank and years of service.)

Given the inherent variation in costs that are attributable in no small measure to personnel expenditures, are there other variables that contribute to variation in costs across institutions, *within* a given discipline? Middaugh et al. (2003) found that between 60 and 75 percent of the cost variation within a discipline, depending on the discipline, is associated with the following factors:

- The volume of teaching activity, measured in terms of student credit hours taught. Consistent with economies of scale, the more student credit hours taught by a faculty of fixed size, the lower the cost.
- Department size, measured in terms of the total number of faculty: the larger the department, the greater the cost.
- The proportion of faculty holding tenure. Because tenured faculty tend to be compensated at higher levels than nontenurable faculty at the same institution, and because they are "fixed costs" (remaining with the institution until retirement or resignation), the higher the tenure rate, the greater the expense.

- Although the presence of graduate-level instruction had a positive association with increased instructional expenditures, the measurable effect of this variable on cost was far smaller than the effect of the volume of teaching, departmental size, and tenure rate.

- Similarly, the extent to which disciplines are equipment intensive (for example, physical sciences and engineering) produced a positive measurable association with cost; however, the magnitude of that association fell far short of that for teaching volume, department size, and tenure rate.

So what do the aforementioned findings say to the individual wishing to increase productivity and reduce instructional costs within a discipline? The draconian solution would be to increase the number of student credit hours taught and have them taught by a smaller number of faculty, none of whom are tenured. If all that faculty did at an institution was teach, this solution might merit at least some discussion. But as anyone who has spent a day on a college or university campus knows, the spectrum of activities in which faculty engage and are expected to engage as part of the promotion and tenure process goes well beyond just teaching. The difficulty is that higher education, as a collective entity, has done a miserable job of communicating the full range of faculty engagement at an institution. When institutions have attempted such conversation, all too often the focus is on how faculty allocate their time, as opposed to a discussion of the output or products of faculty activity.

A More Complete Picture of Faculty Productivity

Over the past two decades, the Delaware Study of Instructional Costs and Productivity has emerged as the state-of-the-art data sharing consortium for benchmarking detailed information on faculty teaching loads, instructional costs, and externally funded scholarship. As noted earlier, externally funded research and service expenditures provide a useful proxy when examining teaching loads and instructional costs. Where teaching activity is low and instructional costs are high in comparison with national benchmarks, one would look for high volume research and service expenditures as context for the productivity and cost measures. The problem is that many disciplines—most notably the fine arts and humanities—do not attract external funding in the same fashion as the sciences and engineering. Yet faculty in these disciplines are still expected to engage in scholarly activity and service as a prerequisite to promotion and tenure. How, then, can this information be captured as context data for Delaware Study productivity and cost measures?

Aware of these limitations, the University of Delaware again approached FIPSE in 2000 for a second grant to support the Delaware Study. Following the model used to develop the data collection form for the teaching load/cost portion of the Delaware Study, a new advisory committee was convened to develop instrumentation and a data collection methodology for assessing out-of-classroom faculty activity. Whereas the teaching load/cost advisory committee members were mainly institutional researchers and higher education economists, the out-of-classroom faculty activity advisory committee members were deans and faculty who routinely either engage in or assess such activity. The decision was made to focus the data collection on activities related to instruction, scholarship, and service. Service was broadly defined to include service to the institution, to the profession, and public service. When assessing institutional effectiveness, it is important to understand the full scope of faculty activity and how one institution compares to national benchmarks for peer institutions. The objective is to determine the extent to which an institution is making the most effective use of one of its core resources—that is, its faculty.

Discussion among the members of the advisory committee began to focus on a number of key faculty activities that could and should be measured across institutions. These included the following:

- *Instruction*: academic advising; thesis and dissertation supervision; curriculum design and redesign; supervision of clinical courses, internships, cooperative education courses, and the like

- *Scholarship:* Refereed and nonrefereed publications, juried shows and commissioned performances, patents issued, software development, web-based learning modules, and the like
- *Service:* Service on institutional committees, extension and outreach activity, service to professional associations, and the like

The resulting data collection form is displayed in Exhibit 6.1. Actually collecting the data in the Exhibit 6.1 form is not as straightforward as the data collection associated with teaching loads and costs. The latter category of data are typically found in the institution's course registration and financial databases. The data associated with out-of-classroom faculty activity are more typically found in a file cabinet in the department chair's office. The problem of noncentralized faculty activity data was compounded by the potential perception that the Delaware Study was examining the activities of individual faculty. Consequently, beginning with the initial data collection in 2002, great care was taken to underscore that the Delaware Study was collecting data at the departmental level of aggregation and had no interest in individual faculty data other than having it rolled up and reported at that aggregate level.

Institutions participating in the faculty activity portion of the Delaware Study are encouraged to collect the information in the Exhibit 6.1 form at that point during the academic year when annual performance reviews are conducted. The data elements in the data collection form are precisely the foci of conversations taking place during the performance evaluation. Consequently, it is a relatively simple matter for a department chair to complete a checklist for each faculty member that is identical to Exhibit 6.1 and to have a clerical staffer or graduate student aggregate the data.

A number of institutions are moving toward electronic collection of data on faculty activity. Commercial vendors provide data

Exhibit 6.1 Delaware Study of Instructional Costs and Productivity

Institution: FICE Code:

Discipline: CIP Code:

Degrees Offered in Discipline (check all that apply): ___Bachelor's ___ Master's ___ Doctorate ___ Professional

This study focuses on the discipline level of analysis. Please carefully consult the data definitions accompanying this data collection form before reporting information. All data should be reported for the most recent 12-month faculty evaluation period as defined in the instructions. Please denote any not-applicable data as "na" and any data element that is truly zero as "0".

Discipline-Specific Statistics

A. Total full-time equivalent (FTE) tenured faculty.___

B. Total FTE tenure-track faculty.___

C. Total FTE tenured and tenure-track faculty on which your responses below will be based.___

Activities Related to Teaching

1. Total number of separate course preparations faculty have developed.___

2. Number of existing courses where faculty have redesigned the pedagogy or curriculum under the auspices of a grant or course-release time.___

3. Number of new courses which faculty have created and delivered.___

4. Number of courses indicated in the previous item which are delivered fully or primarily online.___

5. Unduplicated headcount of undergraduate academic advisees formally assigned to faculty.___

6. Unduplicated headcount of graduate academic advisees formally assigned to faculty.___

7. Number of thesis/dissertation committees where faculty served as chairperson.___

8. Number of thesis/dissertation committees where faculty served in a non-chairing role.___

9. Number of undergraduate senior theses (e.g., senior thesis, recital, art show, other capstone experiences) that faculty have advised.___

10. Total number of students taught individually in independent or directed studies (e.g., one-on-one student faculty interaction for credit directed as satisfying a degree requirement).___

11. Number of undergraduate students formally engaged in research with a faculty mentor.___

Exhibit 6.1 (Continued)

12. Number of graduate students formally engaged in research with a faculty mentor.___

13. Number of clinical students (e.g., student nurses), practicum students (e.g., student teachers), internship students, and students in cooperative and service learning education programs who are formally assigned to faculty.___

14. Number of students (undergraduate and graduate) who have co-authored a journal article or book chapter with a faculty mentor.___

15. Number of students (undergraduate and graduate) who have co-presented a paper at a state, regional, national, and international professional meeting with a faculty mentor.___

16. Number of assessment projects or separate assignments for purpose of program evaluation (as distinct from individual courses) faculty have undertaken.___

17. Number of institution-sanctioned professional development activities related to teaching efforts (e.g., workshops offered by Center for Teaching Effectiveness).___

Activities Related to Scholarship

18. Number of print or electronic refereed journal articles, book chapters, and creative works published by faculty.___

19. Number of print or electronic non-refereed journal articles, book chapters, and creative works published by faculty.___

20. Number of single-author or joint-author books or monographs written by faculty and published by an academic or commercial press.___

21. Number of manuscripts (e.g., journal articles, books) submitted to publishers.___

22. Number of books, collections, and monographs edited by faculty.___

23. Number of books, journal articles, and manuscripts reviewed and formally submitted by faculty.___

24. Number of editorial positions held by faculty.___

25. Number of juried shows, commissioned performances, creative readings, and competitive exhibitions by faculty.___

26. Number of non-juried shows, performances, creative readings, and exhibitions by faculty.___

27. Number of digital programs or applications (e.g., software development, web-based learning modules) designed by faculty related to field of expertise.___

(continued)

Exhibit 6.1   (Continued)

28. Number of provisional or issued patents based on faculty products.___

29. Number of faculty works in progress (e.g., journal articles, paintings, musical compositions).___

30. Number of formal presentations made by faculty at state, regional, national, and international professional meetings.___

31. Number of external and institutionally-designated grant, contract, and scholarly fellowship proposals submitted by faculty.___

32. Number of new external grants, contracts, and scholarly fellowships formally awarded to faculty or to the institution on behalf of faculty.___

33. Total dollar value of the new externally funded grants, contracts, and scholarly fellowships which you reported in Item 32.___

34. Number of new institutionally-designated grants and contracts formally awarded to faculty.___

35. Total dollar value of the new institutionally-designated grants and contracts which you reported in Item 34.___

36. Number of continuing external and institutionally-designated grants, contracts, and scholarly fellowships.___

37. Number of institution-sanctioned professional development activities related to scholarship. ___

Activities Related to Service

38. Number of faculty activities related to institutional service (e.g., faculty governance, faculty committees, peer mentoring, academic programs in residences, recruiting efforts, student activity advisor, other student activity involvement).___

39. Number of faculty extension and outreach activities related to field of expertise (e.g., civic service, K–12 service, community workshops, invited talks to community groups, seminars, lectures, demonstrations).___

40. Number of faculty activities related to recognized or visible service to profession (e.g., service on a regional or national committee, service on a self-study visitation team for another institution, serving as a volunteer juror for a show, performance, or exhibition).___

41. Number of grant proposals reviewed by faculty related to field of expertise.___

42. Number of leadership positions in a professional association held by faculty (e.g., elected officer, committee chairperson, conference chair).___

collection templates and software. Institutions that lack the resources, time, or both to pursue the commercially developed options can download copies of briefing papers on best practices in faculty activity data collection from the Delaware Faculty Activity Study website at http://www.udel.edu/IR/focs/. The briefing papers address both institutionally developed electronic data collection processes and hardcopy data collections. The electronic processes are particularly impressive in their elegance, simplicity, and relatively low cost to develop. Having such information readily available to institutional decision makers enhances the likelihood of effective deployment of faculty resources.

Benchmarking Out-of-Classroom Faculty Activity

Participation in the early cycles of the faculty activity portion of the Delaware Study has been less robust than the teaching load/cost portion, due largely to the methodological issues just described. Although the teaching load/cost data collection annually draws 200 to 250 institutions, the faculty activity data collection draws between 50 and 75 institutions. As that portion of the Delaware Study receives wider attention, particularly in light of demands from accrediting bodies for measures of institutional effectiveness with respect to how faculty spend their time, participation can be expected to increase. In the meantime, there are still useful measures to be derived from analyzing the data.

Figure 6.5 examines national benchmark data for English faculty engaged in selected variables related to instruction. In calculating national benchmarks for the faculty activity portion of the Delaware Study, the decision was made to use median values as opposed to mean values as a more reliable measure of central tendency, given the smaller number of participating institutions and the even smaller N's within a given discipline. Figure 6.5 reports the median number of instances reported per FTE Faculty for five variables related to out-of-classroom instructional activity; namely, the number of

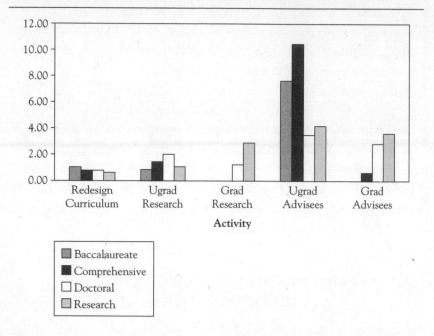

Figure 6.5 Faculty Activity in Selected Dimensions of Instructional Activity: English

- Courses for which the curriculum was redesigned
- Undergraduate students formally engaged in research with faculty
- Graduate students engaged in research
- Undergraduate advisees formally assigned to faculty
- Graduate advisees

The data are arrayed by Carnegie classification of reporting institution. Regardless of Carnegie classification, redesign of curricula is evident, as is undergraduate research activity. Graduate research activity, not surprisingly, is reported at doctoral and research institutions. Undergraduate advising loads are heaviest at baccalaureate and comprehensive institutions, where they encompass most of the student body, whereas graduate advising loads are heaviest at doctoral and research universities. These data enable participating institutions to assess which instructional activities are in play at the home institution and the magnitude of those activities in comparison with preliminary national benchmarks—preliminary because of the evolving levels of institutional participation in this portion of the Delaware Study.

Figure 6.6 examines selected dimensions of scholarly activity. Publication activity is heaviest at research and doctoral institutions, where such activity is an explicit requirement for promotion and tenure. The same could be said for grant activity, although it is worthy of note that this activity occurs at comprehensive institutions as well, albeit in far smaller proportions. That said, it is still important to describe the full scope of faculty activity when discussing how faculty actually utilize their time.

Figure 6.7 examines activity related to institutional, professional, and public service. What is striking about the data is the

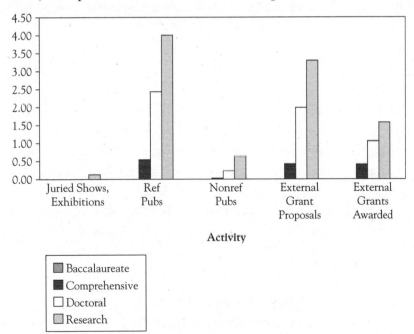

Figure 6.6 Faculty Activity in Selected Dimensions of Scholarship Activity: English

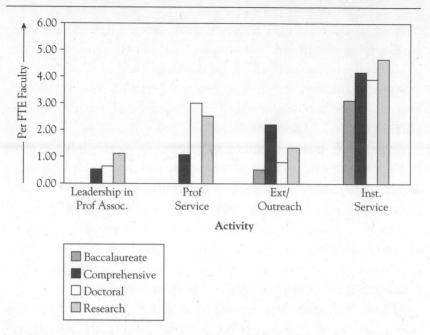

Figure 6.7 Faculty Activity in Selected Dimensions of Service Activity: English

number of instances of institutional service per FTE faculty, regardless of institutional Carnegie classification. Other forms of service activity are also in evidence, although in varying amounts across institutional type.

Data analyses of out-of-classroom faculty activity are important because this enables a more complete portrait of how faculty resources are being utilized. The emphasis throughout this book has been on measuring institutional effectiveness. The more complete the basis on which those assessments are made, the better the measures of institutional effectiveness.

Some Final Thoughts on Delaware Study Benchmarking

When thinking about how much faculty teach, how much that instruction costs, and the extent to which those two measures are mitigated by other things that faculty do, it is certainly important to have consistent and reliable data that describe actual practices at a given institution. Strategies for building such measures for teaching loads and costs were thoroughly discussed in Chapter Five. And blueprints for building databases that document the full range of faculty activity are evident in the briefing papers, cited in this chapter, on the out-of-classroom faculty activity website for the Delaware Study.

A recurring theme throughout this book is the importance of having contextual benchmark data when describing institutional effectiveness. Certainly, discrete institutional measures have value when looking at the effectiveness and efficiency of institutional operations. But those measures become even more powerful and useful when cast within the context of similar measures from actual and aspirational peer institutions. As noted at the beginning of this chapter, assessing institutional effectiveness with regard to instructional activity and cost is best done at the academic discipline level of analysis. Because the Delaware Study of Instructional Cost and Productivity and its two-year institutional counterpart, the Kansas Study of Instructional Costs and Productivity, are the only national data sharing consortia that collect this information at the discipline level, they are important tools in any attempt to truly assess institutional effectiveness.

Over the past two decades, the Delaware Study of Instructional Productivity has witnessed significant increases in the number of participating institutions. It can thus be projected that, given accreditation demands for evidence of institutional effectiveness, the Kansas Study of Instructional Costs and Productivity will experience similar growth within the two-year college sector. Among four-year institutions, the Delaware Study has been embraced as the tool of choice for assessing instructional workload and costs by data sharing consortia such as the Association of American Universities Data Exchange (AAUDE) and the Southern Universities Group (SUG). A decade ago, participation by liberal arts baccalaureate institutions was somewhat limited. However, following a series of Delaware Study workshops presented to the Chief Academic

Officers group within the Council of Independent Colleges (CIC), the baccalaureate institution sector has enjoyed vigorous annual participation. Whole systems are seeing the value of interinstitutional benchmarking at the academic discipline level of analysis. The Tennessee Higher Education Commission (THEC), the University of North Carolina System, and the University of Missouri System are long-standing members of the Delaware Study. The University of North Carolina System has found Delaware Study data to be particularly useful in funding discussions with the state legislature by providing a comparative context from other states with respect to the measures developed for North Carolina institutions.

Chapters Five and Six have focused on measures of institutional effectiveness intended to look at the deployment of human and fiscal resources in support of teaching and learning. Naturally, the focus has been on academic units. What about institutional effectiveness within administrative units? That is the focus of discussion in Chapter Seven.

7

MEASURING ADMINISTRATIVE EFFECTIVENESS

Approaching assessment of administrative effectiveness is considerably more difficult than measuring the effectiveness of academic units. In considering instructional productivity, costs, and overall effectiveness, there is a common coin of the realm: the student credit hour. Technically referred to as a Carnegie Unit, the student credit hour is a commonly defined measure of the time that students spend in study in a given course. A student credit hour means the same thing in chemistry as it does in anthropology, and it has the same value at one institution as it does at any other college or university in the United States.

There is no such common measure in administrative activity, and this has confounded attempts at benchmarking activity within administrative units both within a given institution and across institutional boundaries. Over the years there have been attempts to benchmark administrative productivity, but none has been particularly successful. This is due in large part to the nature of administrative functions and the difficulty in quantifying them. Transactional measures such as the number of admissions applications or completed registrations processed per professional staff member in the admissions or registrar's office presuppose a commonality in the manner in which students are admitted to an institution or in how they register for courses. And although there may be some functional commonality, there are also real differences. Computing and software systems vary from institution to institution, as do administrative procedures.

To illustrate this point, consider the admissions process at the University of Delaware. For years, the University used what is referred to as a "predicted grade index" (PGI) to make a first pass at a decision on whether or not to admit a student to undergraduate study; this is a common practice in admissions offices across the country. The predicted grade index is a multiple regression equation into which are entered a student's high school grades on core academic courses (science, mathematics, social studies, languages, and so on), and the equation predicts the college grade point average at the end of the first term of University study based on historical correlations. Specific cutoff points in predicted grade indices determined whether students would be given further consideration in the admissions process. However, the University began to notice substantial variation in grading practices at feeder high schools, calling into question the effectiveness of the PGI's predictive usefulness; in 2000 they decided to move from the PGI and to instead require a written essay from all applicants, intended to demonstrate the ability to integrate and synthesize complex ideas and arguments, as a more effective and reliable predictor of college success. At the time this decision was being made, applications for admission to the University had increased from thirteen thousand in 1994–95 to well in excess of twenty thousand in 2000–01. Benchmarking the number of processed admissions applications per professional staff member might make sense among institutions, with all using the PGI. But when the required essay is introduced, the process becomes more complex, as each applicant essay has to be read. It is further complicated when an institution is experiencing a significant increase in the number of applications, such as that seen at the University of Delaware. Clearly, any comparison between PGI institutions and the University of Delaware would be virtually meaningless. Given the complexity of making comparisons among specific administrative units, how might an institution approach the issue of assessing administrative effectiveness? Taylor and Massy (1996) argued that the effectiveness of an institution lies in its ability to strategically respond to circumstances, and that capability to respond can actually be quantified.

It's In the Numbers

Specifically, Taylor and Massy suggest ten key indicators that speak to institutional functioning and viability. A quick review of those indicators will prove instructive.

1. *Revenue Structure:* It is important to understand the various revenue streams contributing to the institution's budget and to monitor the relative dependence on a given revenue stream over time. Tuition dependency is a real issue for many colleges. Among small colleges with minimal endowments, it is not uncommon to find that two-thirds to three-fourths, and occasionally more, of total revenues to the institution come from tuition. At institutions such as these, a stable tuition revenue stream is an indirect measure of the effectiveness of both admissions and student life units. Highly effective institutions diversify revenue streams to the greatest extent possible and monitor key revenue streams such as tuition for stability and reliability. Dramatic variation in the annual relative contribution of various revenue streams suggests an institution faced with uncertainty as the result of inability to manage those revenue streams. Specific strategies for understanding and monitoring revenue structure will be described later in this chapter. Particularly important is the capacity both to monitor internal revenue streams and to benchmark their relative contribution to the total budget compared with appropriate peer institutions.

2. *Expenditure Structure:* As important as it is to understand how money flows into a college or university, it is equally important to understand and monitor how it is being spent. Are spending patterns at the institution consistent and stable with respect to

the proportion of education and general expenditures (the basic cost of doing business) allocated to instruction? Academic support? Student services? Financial aid? Administrative functions? Spikes in any given expenditure category occasionally occur. But incremental growth over time within any given category should raise questions about the underlying causes for that growth. As with revenues, it is important to both internally monitor and externally benchmark the relative impact of each expenditure category on total institutional spending. The objective is to ensure that resources are being spent in a fashion consistent with the institution's core mission.

3. *Excess (Deficit) of Current Fund Revenues over Current Fund Expenditures*: This measure examines the extent to which the volume of revenue exceeds or falls short of the volume of expenditure. Obviously the goal is to have larger revenues than expenditures, and such a measure is a rough indicator of how long a given institution could operate without additional revenues. The more effective the institution, the larger the excess revenue. When Taylor and Massy (1996) wrote their book, they argued that this measure was meaningful only to private institutions, as public institutions are frequently prohibited from accumulating fund balances. At that time, they suggested that public colleges and universities monitor measures such as state appropriation as a percentage of education and general expenditures, state appropriation per FTE student, and so on. However, in the decade that followed publication of the book, state support for higher education has significantly declined in most states, and "public" college and university revenue streams are increasingly mimicking those of private institutions, including greater dependence on tuition and fees. Thus the excess/deficit revenue measure is taking on increasing relevance for public institutions as well.

4. *Percentage of Freshman Applicants Accepted and Percentage of Accepted Applicants Who Enroll*: The first of these measures is an

indicator of institutional selectivity; the higher the offer rate, the less selective the institution. Although open enrollment or near-open enrollment is a legitimate facet of the institutional mission for some colleges and universities, it also creates significant issues when it comes to managing enrollment and providing the appropriate academic and student support services needed to enhance the prospects of student success. That is not to say that open enrollment institutions cannot be effective. It does suggest, however, that all of the strategies discussed in earlier chapters relative to measuring student needs, student satisfaction, and student engagement become particularly crucial for institutions of this type. The second measure, commonly referred to as the "yield rate," is an indicator of how attractive the institution is within the admissions marketplace. The higher the yield rate, the more desirable the institution is to prospective institutions. It is reasonable to assume that the attractiveness of an institution is due, in no small measure, to the extent to which the college or university is perceived to effectively meet the full range of academic and other needs of students.

5. *Ratio of Full-Time Equivalent Students to Full-Time Equivalent Faculty:* Taylor and Massy emphasize the importance of assessing faculty workloads as an indicator of institutional effectiveness. The ability to do so at the academic discipline level of analysis was fully described in Chapter Five of this book, and the ability to benchmark workload measures across institutions in Chapter Six.

6. *Institutional Scholarship and Fellowship Expenditures as a Percentage of Total Tuition and Fees Income:* Also known as tuition discounting, this is a measure of the extent to which institutions use tuition and fees revenue to subsidize the cost of attending that institution. Colleges and universities in general can and must use financial aid as a tool for attracting and retaining students; the actual level of tuition discounting is an important measure, particularly for highly tuition dependent

institutions. The higher the level of tuition discounting, the lower the availability of tuition and fees to support institutional expenditures other than financial aid, and the more compelling the need to rapidly diversify revenue streams, a difficult task for many institutions. Although the objective might be to attract the largest possible number of full-paying students, the reality is that need-based and merit-based financial aid is essential to attracting and retaining students. Consequently, enrollment management strategies must include careful consideration of tuition discounting practices.

7. *Tenure Status of Full-Time Equivalent Faculty*: This indicator examines the proportion of FTE faculty who hold tenure. The higher the tenure rate, the less flexible the institution can be in bringing in new faculty within a fixed instructional budget. This impedes the ability to add new programs or to enhance existing programs to meet increasing student demand. As noted in Chapter Six, colleges and universities are achieving some measure of flexibility as tenured faculty retire or resign by creating full-time, nontenurable faculty lines whose sole function is teaching.

8. *Percent of Total Full-Time Equivalent Employees Who Are Faculty*: This is an important indicator that must be carefully and appropriately interpreted. A high percentage of full-time employees designated as faculty can be representative of one of two scenarios: either the institution is emphasizing the academic facet of the institutional mission and is staffing up to support teaching, research, and service, or the institution is not appropriately staffed in a manner that fully supports administrative and other nonacademic functions essential to effective functioning, and faculty are being asked to assume multiple roles. Consequently, depending on the interpretation of this measure, a high faculty percentage of full-time employees is a measure of either institutional effectiveness or inefficiency.

9. *Estimated Maintenance Backlog as a Percentage of the Replacement Value of Plant*: Deferred maintenance seriously jeopardizes institutional effectiveness and efficiency. Money spent on addressing serious issues of deferred maintenance represents resources no longer available for functions central to the institutional mission. Sooner or later, deferred maintenance becomes essential maintenance. So the higher the proportion of deferred maintenance as characterized in this indicator, the greater the potential drain on institutional resources. Some institutions defer maintenance to the point where it becomes more cost-effective to demolish the structure and replace it. However, the replacement funds are then not available for other institutional purposes. A simple rule of thumb for highly effective institutions is that they annually set aside at least 2 percent of the replacement value of the physical plant to be used for facilities renewal and renovation. The underlying assumption for this rule is that the projected life span for most college and university buildings is fifty years. Annually setting aside 2 percent of the replacement value for those buildings over the course of fifty years generates sufficient resources to totally eliminate deferred maintenance and put the campus on a cycle of planned maintenance. Although this rule of thumb may seem like an exceedingly ambitious goal for an institution, the closer a college or university comes to achieving it, the less deferred maintenance will erode institutional effectiveness. That this can be achieved was evident in the University of Delaware strategic planning case study in Chapter Two.

10. *Percent of Living Alumni Who Have Given at Any Time During the Past Five Years*: The extent to which alumni choose to financially support their alma mater may be viewed as an assessment of their satisfaction with both the quality and the effectiveness of programs and services available to them during their college careers.

The Taylor and Massy strategic indicators provide broad-brush measures of institutional performance and are a basis for framing more specific questions related to the effectiveness of the full range of institutional services.

A Bit More on Institutional Finances

The monitoring of institutional revenues and expenditures suggested by Taylor and Massy (1996), and described in the preceding section on strategic indicators, does indeed require a fundamental understanding of higher education finance. If lawyers are guilty of creating a foreign language, "legalese," accountants are no less culpable with their "accountancy-speak." Essentially, higher education finance is split into two camps—those using accounting standards promulgated by the Governmental Accounting Standards Board (GASB)—primarily public institutions—and those put forward by the Financial Accounting Standards Board (FASB)—primarily private or independently chartered institutions. Each of the two accounting boards has its own definitions and procedures for booking revenues and expense within the institutional budget, and they are sufficiently different that, as of this writing, ratio analysis financial benchmarks among institutions should be made only within each respective set of accounting standards.

Acknowledging the differences in accounting standards between public and private institutions, it is still possible to monitor and benchmark the Taylor and Massy strategic indicators separately between GASB and FASB institutions, respectively. A college or university has certain fundamental revenue streams, regardless of how they are accounted for. These include the following:

- Tuition and mandatory fees
- Contracts and grants
- Governmental appropriations
- Gifts
- Income from endowment and temporary investments

- Auxiliary operations
- Other revenues

Colleges and universities also have fundamental expense categories, including these:

- Instruction and department research
- Sponsored research
- Extension and public service
- Academic support
- Student services
- General institutional support
- Operations and maintenance of physical plant
- Student aid

The sum of these expense categories is referred to as "total education and general expenditures" and reflects the cost of doing business at a higher education institution; that is, expenses incurred in functions related to the core mission areas of teaching, research, and service. Expenditures for auxiliary activities (such as dining, residence life, bookstore) are not viewed as core mission functions and are intended to be self-supporting; that is, the revenues from auxiliary activities are expected to fund the full cost of those activities. When expenses from auxiliary enterprises are added to education and general expense, the result is referred to as "total operating expense" for the institution. Table 7.1 displays revenues and expenses at the University of Delaware in FY 2007.

In monitoring revenue streams, a simple ratio calculation is used:

$$\frac{\text{Individual Revenue Stream}}{\text{Total Education and General Expenditures}}$$

Table 7-1   University of Delaware Statement of Revenues and Expense: FY 2007

	(Thousands of Dollars)
Operating Revenue	
Tuition and Fees (Less Scholarships and Fellowships)	219,900
Contributions	19,766
Contracts and Other Exchange Transactions	129,586
State Operating Appropriation	122,828
Endowment Spending Payout	45,869
Other Investment Payout	12,396
Activities of Educational Departments	7,152
Sales and Services of Auxiliary Enterprises (Less Scholarships and Fellowships)	81,818
Other Revenue	14,736
Net Assets Released from Restrictions	0
Operating Expenses	
Education and General:	
Instruction and Departmental Research	279,293
Sponsored Research	103,425
Extension and Public Service	40,492
Academic Support	54,900
Student Services	22,202
General Institutional Support	57,985
Student Aid	6,144
Reclassification of Funds	−1,013
Total Education and General Expenses	563,428
Auxiliary Enterprises	76,209

For example, in its Fiscal Year 2007 Annual Financial report, the University of Delaware reported income from tuition and fees totaling $219.9 million, and education and general expenditures totaling $563.4 million. Using the ratio just noted (tuition and fees/education and general expenditures), tuition and fees at the

University support 39 percent of education and general expense. The ratio can be calculated using any of the revenue streams just listed. During FY 2007, contracts and grants at the University of Delaware totaled $129.8 million. Plugging that figure into the ratio, it can be discerned that contracts and grants support 23 percent of education and general expense at the University.

In monitoring these and other revenue streams, it is important to look at the ratios for each revenue stream over time to determine the stability or instability of that revenue source. If, over time, the tuition and fees ratio is declining, it is important to understand the underlying reasons. If the decline is due to a steady increase in the relative contribution of contracts and grants or gift income, that is a good indicator, signaling increased research activity, increased activity in institutional fund raising, or both— and both are positive measures of administrative institutional effectiveness. If the decline is due to a decrease in student enrollment, with all other revenue streams holding steady, enrollment management practices need to be reviewed. On the other hand, if the tuition and fees ratio increases, it is important to understand why that is the case as well. If it is the result of a planned increase in student enrollment or the result of a planned, systematic increase in tuition revenues, that may be a positive indicator, although it does call for careful monitoring of its impact on retention and graduation rates. But if analysis of the respective contribution of each revenue stream to education and general expense over time suggests that the increase in the tuition and fees is due to a decline in the relative contribution of the other revenue streams, it is time to examine the effectiveness of the research office, development office, or other administrative units responsible for generating the respective revenue streams.

As important as it is to monitor revenue streams as broad gauges of institutional effectiveness, it is equally important to monitor how resources are being spent; this is usually referred to as an examination of expenditure demand. Once again, ratio analysis is the analytical vehicle, with education and general expenditures continuing as the divisor.

$$\frac{\text{Individual Expenditure Category}}{\text{Total Education and General Expenditures}}$$

In FY 2007, the University of Delaware spent $279.3 million on instruction and departmental research. Using the preceding ratio, that expenditure category represented 49.6 percent of all education and general expenditures; the $103.4 million spent on sponsored research was 18.3 percent of education and general expense, the $58.0 million on general institutional support (translate that as general administrative services) was 10.3 percent, and so on. As was the case with revenues, it is important to monitor each categorical expenditure ratio over time. Keeping in mind that the central mission of most colleges and universities centers on some configuration of teaching, research, and service, the objective is to examine the extent to which each of the expenditure categories is functioning in a manner that contributes to the institution's mission. If the institution is a community college or baccalaureate institution, one would expect the expenditure demand ratios for instruction and department research and academic support to significantly outpace other ratios. Conversely, at research universities, one might reasonably expect the instruction and academic support ratios to be smaller than those seen at two-year and baccalaureate institutions, while the ratios for sponsored research and extension and public research would be far more evident. And at all institutions, it is important to monitor the extent to which noncore mission ratios—such as general institutional support (administrative services) and operation and maintenance of physical plant—are systematically increasing over time, potentially siphoning resources from core mission areas. Expenditure demand ratios provide a context for framing broad questions about the general institutional effectiveness of administrative offices.

As useful as revenue contribution and expenditure demand analyses are in framing questions about institutional effectiveness at a single college or university, those ratios become even more useful when viewed against comparable ratios at appropriate peer institutions. The Integrated Postsecondary Educational Data System (IPEDS) is a major annual data collection conducted by the National Center for Education Statistics. It comprises a number of annual surveys—Institutional Characteristics, Fall Enrollment, Completions, Graduation Rate Survey, and so on. A central survey in the IPEDS series is the yearly Finance Survey, which requires institutions to submit information on revenues and expenditures, by category, consistent with their FASB or GASB guidelines. IPEDS maintains an online database reflecting institutional submissions of each of their surveys. The database is accessible online, using the IPEDS Peer Analysis tool (http://nces.ed.gov/ipedspas). Users of the Peer Analysis tool can then select both peer institutions for comparison purposes and specific variables from the Finance Survey to calculate both revenue contribution and expenditure demand ratios for each of those selected peers. This enables institutions to gauge their own performance over time and to compare it with the performance of appropriate peer institutions. One cautionary note: because of the differences in reporting between institutions using FASB and those using GASB accounting standards, it is best not to benchmark across the two types of institutions. At this writing, NCES is working toward reconciliation between FASB and GASB requirements on the Finance Survey. That has not happened yet, and until it does, FASB and GASB colleges and universities should remain within their respective families of institutions.

Other Strategies for Assessing Administrative Effectiveness

It is possible to obtain benchmark data on specific performance indicators within certain administrative functional areas. For example, the Association of Physical Plant Administrators (APPA) regularly conducts a Facilities Performance Indicators

Survey, the results from which are extremely valuable to institutions working toward best practice in facilities administration. The College and University Professional Association for Human Resources (CUPA-HR; http://www.cupahr.org/) annually collects salary information for senior-level and mid-level college and university administrators that is position-specific, as well as faculty salary information, by academic rank and discipline. These data are critical to ensuring that institutions are market-competitive when hiring. The National Association of College and University Business Officers (NACUBO; www.nacubo.org) annually produces a series of research reports designed to enhance business practices and finance administration at postsecondary institutions. Readers of this volume should check with their own professional association to determine the availability of resources on performance indicators in their specific field.

A highly effective means of assessing institutional effectiveness is to simply ask the end users how satisfied they are with products and services from specific administrative units. Student satisfaction surveys have long been used to assess the extent to which admission, financial aid, registration, and accounts payable functions, among others, are addressing specific needs of students. The University of Delaware uses the ACT Survey of Student Opinions as a general diagnostic tool to identify areas of student discontent, then applies a more focused data collection to identify appropriate remedial strategies. Specifically, they have developed a series of web-based Campus Pulse Surveys, containing fifteen to twenty issue-specific items that can be quickly completed. Students are notified of the surveys by e-mail and are directed to the appropriate web address.

Two illustrative examples of Campus Pulse activity, briefly highlighted in Chapter Four, merit further elaboration here. As a result of information gleaned from the Survey of Student Opinions, the University sought more detailed information on student dissatisfaction with academic advising and student registration procedures. Students had indicated a general dissatisfaction with academic advising. When probed via a Campus Pulse Survey, the specific areas of dissatisfaction that emerged centered on the availability of advisors and the quality of information being dispensed to freshmen—and to a lesser extent sophomores with undeclared majors—primarily on which courses should be taken to satisfy general education requirements. Juniors and seniors tended to be generally satisfied with the information from faculty advisors, once majors were declared and advanced study was underway. This led the University to develop a University Advisement Center, with a faculty director and a professional advising staff, specifically tailored to meeting the needs of students who have not yet decided on a specific field of study. Another example of Campus Pulse activity, referenced earlier in Chapter Four, centered on student dissatisfaction with registration procedures that coincided with implementation of a new web-based administrative software system. In this instance, the dissatisfaction was concentrated largely among juniors and seniors who had acquired familiarity and a comfort level with registering for courses under the old mainframe-based software and were having problems adjusting to the web-based software. Freshmen and sophomores, who had known no software other than the web-based software, were quite content with registration procedures. Consequently, rather than make drastic adjustments to the course registration process, the University focused on assisting students with difficulties in registering, knowing that as younger students progressed through their studies, the problem would ultimately resolve itself.

In addition to surveying students, many institutions have programs of systematic review of administrative units akin to the methodology used in academic program review and accreditation. Administrative units are required to engage in self-study and produce a report detailing the unit's mission, goals, and objectives and how those relate to the larger mission and goals of the institution. External reviewers are often used to assess the quality and outcomes of the unit self-study.

Conclusions

Although assessing the effectiveness of administrative units is perhaps not as straightforward as the procedures used to measure productivity and effectiveness in academic disciplines, it is neither a daunting nor an impossible task. Using a combination of the strategies outlined in this chapter, as well as a good dose of common sense, colleges and universities can develop and implement a systematic set of strategies for assessing administrative effectiveness. And those strategies should be a central component of assessing overall institutional effectiveness.

8

COMMUNICATING
ASSESSMENT RESULTS

This chapter is about *information*. The word is emphasized because all too often the products of assessment activity fail to undergo an important transformation. Virtually all of the assessment practices discussed in the preceding chapters can be characterized as data analyses in one form or another. A cardinal tenet in communicating assessment results is the basic understanding that *data are not, in and of themselves, equivalent to information*. Data have to be massaged, manipulated, and interpreted to render them into a form of information that is readily digestible and is *used* for planning, decision making, and the allocation of resources. The primary focus of this chapter is the translation of assessment data into usable information for institutional decision makers. A secondary benefit of such translations is that assessment and planning *information* (not data) can then be communicated to external audiences, as appropriate, to describe institutional outcomes.

The author of this volume has been a commissioner with the Middle States Commission on Higher Education for the past several years, serving most recently as vice chair of the Commission. During that time, a consistent pattern has played out among institutions going through institutional self-study and development of periodic review reports relating to compliance with the Commission's fourteen accreditation standards. For the most part, there is no shortage of evidence that the vast majority of the 535 institutions in the Middle States Region are engaged in an array of activities directed at measuring student learning and institutional effectiveness. Although insufficient assessment activity is occasionally the case, where institutions are most likely to encounter problems is in demonstrating that the results from assessment activities are actually being *used* to inform institutional decision making, particularly the institutional strategic planning process.

There are a number of reasons why this is the case. Assessment activities are largely carried out by institutional researchers or by faculty with assistance from institutional researchers. As important as the role of institutional research is at a college or university in gathering data to support assessment initiatives, the simple and stark fact is that there is no formal curriculum or plan of study for training those who enter the institutional research profession, particularly with respect to effective communication of research results. Most institutional researchers come to the profession either from faculty positions or with newly minted degrees (usually master's or doctoral degrees) from programs in which they were taught to do scholarly research.

Although assessment activity certainly has to be grounded in sound research strategies, the primary objective of assessment is to produce *information* (note again the emphasis on information as opposed to data) that can be used for decision making and institutional improvement. The primary objective is *not* the production of a scholarly treatise or refereed journal article describing the technical dimensions of data collection. Institutions, in selecting a commercially prepared survey for assessing student satisfaction or student engagement, trust that the vendor has done all of the necessary calibrations of validity and reliability. The institution is focused on what the survey will tell them about student satisfaction or engagement. The institutional research report that details statistical measures of validity and reliability, confidence intervals, one- or two-tailed tests of significance, and the like will quickly lose the attention of senior management and wind up on a shelf, largely unread. That is not to say that such technical information should not be available if requested. But this request is rarely made. Senior institutional management wants and needs *information* that can be used to shape policy and make decisions. Statistical analyses related to assessment are most often descriptive as opposed to inferential. And much of the research activity related to assessment is ad hoc, relating to information that was needed yesterday and for which a systematic program of inferential research design was never in the cards.

So how do we best develop information—not just data—related to strategic needs and presented in a format with a highly likelihood of use? There are a number of basic guidelines that can guide the process:

1. *Use Charts and Graphs Instead of Numbers.* This has been a recurring theme throughout this book—a picture is worth a thousand numbers! Senior administrators are busy juggling day-to-day crises; they have little time for digesting dense numerical tables crowded with numerical data that make the eyes glaze over. The effective tactic for the assessment office or institutional research office is to capture the attention of a president, provost, or dean with compelling information that prompts follow-up questions. Consider for a moment strategies for presenting information related to the number of undergraduate student credit hours being taught by tenured and tenure-eligible faculty in biology compared with the national benchmark for research universities. The Delaware Study of Instructional Costs and Productivity, discussed in Chapter Six, is an ideal assessment tool for this purpose. Figure 8.1 displays two different strategies for presenting Delaware Study data.

   One might present a data table displaying undergraduate student credit hours taught per FTE tenured and tenure-eligible faculty in all of the departments in the college of arts and science. Are the data any more digestible if only the biology line is displayed? Or one might present the graph shown in Figure 8.1. Which is more likely to get a senior administrator to focus on the volume of undergraduate teaching done by tenured

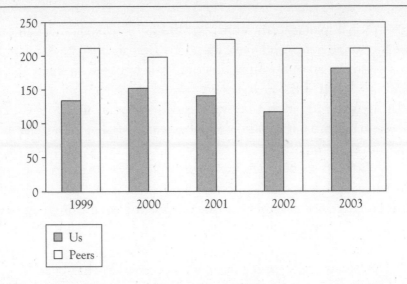

Figure 8.1 Which Is Preferable in Reporting the Trend in Faculty Productivity in the Biology Department with Respect to Undergraduate Teaching Among Tenure-Eligible Faculty?

and tenure-eligible faculty, and to probe the differences from the national benchmark? A pictorial representation of the data quickly isolates the biology department data that are lost in Table 8.1 within Figure 8.1 and easily conveys the *information* that the department consistently teaches below the national benchmark for that discipline.

2. *Remember Your Audience.* As mentioned earlier, although institutional researchers and other professionals who daily use statistical analyses as a tool for understanding similarities and differences among variables will be comfortable with confidence intervals, significance tests, and so on, they must realize that those outside their arena will be less comfortable with—and occasionally confused by—these specialized terms. It is often best, when presenting assessment information to wide audiences, to assume little or no statistical background. Make

Table 8-1 National Study of Instructional Costs and Productivity

Undergraduate Student Credit Hours Taught per FTE Tenured/Tenure-Eligible Faculty

Department	Fall 1999		Fall 2000		Fall 2001		Fall 2002		Fall 2003	
	UD	Nat'l	UD	Nat'l	UD	Nat'l	UD	Nat'l	UD	Nat'l
Anthropology	217	203	253	227	223	208	250	234	274	210
Art	120	157	115	154	87	156	93	154	102	144
Art Conservation	23	157	7	154	19	156	6	154	22	144
Art History	168	157	187	154	193	156	163	154	132	144
Biology	134	211	152	198	141	224	117	210	181	210
Chemistry and Biochemistry	109	230	125	212	125	204	121	217	124	219
Communications	345	206	286	228	265	227	289	228	236	225
Computer and Information Science	97	141	60	136	48	121	39	103	53	86
English	113	128	126	125	128	119	124	129	107	120
Foreign Languages and Literature	93	124	94	115	94	126	87	123	96	127
Geography	259	223	240	223	280	236	253	232	279	250
Geology	286	195	263	197	342	217	293	205	329	197
History	198	220	236	226	207	224	197	238	196	228
Linguistics	168	124	182	115	201	126	208	123	165	127

(continued)

Table 8-1 National Study of Instructional Costs and Productivity (Continued)

Undergraduate Student Credit Hours Taught per FTE Tenured/Tenure-Eligible Faculty

Department	Fall 1999		Fall 2000		Fall 2001		Fall 2002		Fall 2003	
	UD	*Nat'l*	*UD*	*Nat'l*	*UD*	*Nat'l*	*UD*	*Nat'l*	*UD*	*Nat'l*
Mathematical Sciences	146	193	96	191	91	183	88	184	122	179
Music	163	113	166	113	157	118	139	112	132	110
Philosophy	316	233	391	235	418	248	409	237	339	248
Physical Therapy	na	na	na	na	na	na	na	na	na	na
Physics	136	177	87	175	29	173	65	171	124	180
Political Science and International Relations	169	198	236	218	224	223	175	229	218	227
Psychology	388	242	148	255	259	236	267	245	225	243
Sociology and Criminal Justice	216	244	332	249	227	231	205	263	288	251
Theater	65	152	54	129	48	135	45	137	72	135

certain that such technical data are available, if requested, but understand that the technical dimensions of *data* analysis have the capacity to overshadow and obfuscate the *information* that needs to be conveyed.

3. *Statistical Significance.* In a related vein, when examining tests for statistical significance, learn to trust your instincts for examining similarities and differences among variables. Remember at all times that some statistically significant differences in the data are not important, and some important differences may not appear to be statistically significant. When doing student satisfaction studies or campus climate studies, calculation of statistical significance is often a function of the size of the two groups being compared. When looking at student or employee satisfaction scores, for example, based on ethnicity, gender, or sexual orientation, differences may not be statistically significant. But the question that remains to be answered is whether the differences are nonetheless important, representing undertones of potentially larger issues on campus.

Other Communication Strategies

In addition to striving for simplicity and clarity in communicating assessment results, it is good practice to go beyond the simple use of reports in conveying information on institutional effectiveness. Key performance indicators and the use of data dashboards have received considerable publicity in recent years, and they continue to be an effective means of communicating assessment results to a broad range of campus constituencies. A brief review of the steps involved in constructing a campus dashboard is helpful.

Which performance indicators should be used in building the dashboard? The answer depends on the institutional mission of the college or university doing the dashboard construction. For example, the University of Delaware's mission statement reads, in part: "The University affirms its historic mission of providing the highest quality education for its undergraduate students, while maintaining excellence in selected graduate programs. . . . The University will continue to attract and retain the most academically talented and diverse undergraduate students, and support their intellectual, cultural, and ethical development as citizens and scholars." To achieve these mission objectives, the University will have to focus on attracting and retaining the best and most diverse faculty, staff, and students. To do so will require resources, in the form of both faculty compensation and student financial assistance. Consequently, discussion with senior leadership at the University resulted in the decision to focus the dashboard indicators in five areas: admissions, students, faculty, employees, and finances.

In constructing a dashboard, the objective is to assess progress, or lack thereof, in achieving target goals related to selected variables. For admissions, the goals might be achieving a higher yield rate from fewer offers of admission, or substantially increasing the average SAT or ACT score. For students, the goals might include a more diverse student body with higher retention and graduation rates. For faculty and other employees, the institution might seek greater ethnic and gender diversity, with higher levels of compensation. For the area of finances, the institution might wish to monitor demand in various noninstructional expenditure categories with a goal of increasing expenditures on student financial aid. Figure 8.2 displays a portion of the University of Delaware's Dashboard of Key Operational Indicators.

The dashboard is divided into the five categorical headings noted earlier—admissions, students, faculty, employees, and finances. Under each heading are data boxes that display the current values for the variables under examination, as well as the highest and lowest values for those variables within the prior five years. There is also an up arrow or down arrow signaling the direction in which the variable has moved from the prior year, or a blue circle signifying no change. Each of the data boxes gives a quick assessment of relative position of the variable over time. Those wishing greater detail need only click on the chart icon in the center of the data box; a chart appears with more information. Figure 8.3 offers examples of how a user might expand the information in any given data box, displaying the charts that appear when the chart icon is clicked. In the first data box under "Admissions," which deals with the number of first-time freshman applications, we see that there were 21,930 applications in fall 2006, up from the prior year, and that within the five prior years, the high point was 22,208 applications, while the low was 18,209. Similarly, the first data box under "Finances" indicates total operating revenues in the current year totaling $617.1 million, with a high of $585.3 million and a low of $487.7 during the prior five years.

As useful as the dashboard information is in examining trends in key performance indicators over time, a variation on the dashboard that uses peer data is also highly instructive. It is useful to examine data from the U.S. Department of Education's Integrated Postsecondary Education Data System (IPEDS) to develop a set of institutional peers. The IPEDS website has a section devoted to peer analysis, and it offers a series of peer identification tools to assist in identifying institutions comparable to each other. The IPEDS Peer Analysis System can be accessed at http://nces.ed.gov/ipedspas/.

Some institutions may prefer to develop their own peer sets. Such was the case with the University of Delaware in 2007 as it set out on a new strategic planning initiative. Using a statistical tool commonly referred to as cluster analysis, data from the most recent IPEDS data set were examined. Specifically, the analysis focused on a wide range of descriptive institutional variables such as total enrollment, undergraduate/graduate mix, retention and graduation rates, faculty size, total budget, and instructional expenditures. Running these variables through cluster analysis produced two distinctly useful groupings of institutions: those that are actual peers for the University of Delaware, based on institutional characteristics, and a second group of aspirational peers that display institutional characteristics that are goals for the University of Delaware. Figures 8.4 and 8.5, which deal with freshman-to-

Fall 2006

Key

highest value   Current
prior 5 years   Value

1,377	
📊	14,401 ●
1,092	

lowest value
prior 5 years

** Click on chart icon for
6 years of data*

Change from prior year

↑ higher
↓ lower
● no change

Source: 2006/2007 Facts and Figures

Admissions

First-Time Freshman
Applications

22,208	
☐	21,930 ↑
18,209	fall semester

First Time Freshman
Offered Admission

10,256	
☐	10,373 ↑
9,235	fall semester

First-Time Freshman
Paid Deposits

3,522	
☐	3,259 ↓
3,379	

Mean Verbal SAT for
New Freshman

594	
☐	586 ↓
571	

Mean Math SAT for New
Freshman

611	
☐	608 ↓
588	

Mean Combined SAT for
New Freshman

1205	
☐	1194 ↓
1159	

Students

Full-Time Undergraduate
Enrollment Newark
Campus

15,109	
☐	14,400 ↓
14,639	

Percentage of Full Time
Undergraduate Students
Women

59%	
☐	58% ●
58%	

Percentage of Full Time
Undergraduate Students
Minority

16%	
☐	17% ↑
13%	

Percentage of
Undergraduate Students
Delaware Residents

42%	
☐	40% ↓
40%	

Undergraduate Retention
to Second Fall

90%	
☐	90% ↑
89%	

Five-Year Graduation
Rates for Entering Full
Time Freshman

75%	
☐	76% ↑
70%	

**Figure 8.2 University of Delaware Dashboard of Key
Operational Indicators**

Faculty	Employees	Finances

Faculty

Full Time Faculty Counts

1,077	
	1,117 ↑
1,049	

Percentage of Full Time
Faculty Women

37%	
	38% ↑
35%	

Percentage of Full Time
Faculty Minority

15%	
	17% ↑
14%	

Percentage of
Tenure/Tenure Track
Faculty

78%	
	77% ●
76%	

Ratio of FTE Students to
FTE Faculty

13:1	
	12:1 ↓
12:1	

Average Total
Compensation for Full
Time Professors

$147,516	
	$154,733 ↑
$127,300	

Employees

Total Full Time Executive
Employees

378	
	376 ↓
357	

Percentage of Full Time
Executive Employees
Minority

11%	
	9% ●
9%	

Total Full Time
Professional Employees

974	
	953 ↓
814	

Percentage of Full Time
Professional Employees
Women

73%	
	73% ●
70%	

Percentage of Full Time
Professional Employees
Minority

20%	
	18% ↓
16%	

Total Full Time Salaried
and Hourly Employees

1,372	
	1,324 ↑
1,301	

Finances

Total Operating Revenue,
Expenses and Transfers
(Thousands of Dollars)

$585,250	
	$617,154 ↑
$487,749	

Tuition and Fees as
Percentage of Total
Operating Revenue

35.0%	
	34.0% ↓
32.0%	

State Appropriations as
Percentage of Total
Operating Revenue

20.3%	
	19.0% ●
18.5%	

Investments and Gifts as
Percentage of Total
Operating Revenue

13.2%	
	11.0% ●
11.0%	

Instruction and Academic
Support as Percentage of
Total Operating Expenses

52.3%	
	52.0% ●
51.6%	

Sponsored Activities as
Percentage of Total
Operating Expenses

21.0%	
	22.0% ↑
18.1%	

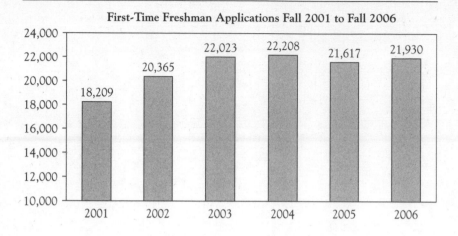

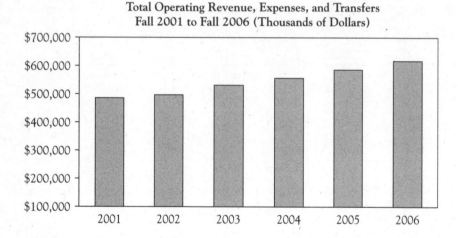

Figure 8.3 Representative Charts Associated with University of Delaware Dashboard Data Boxes

sophomore retention rates and six-year graduation rates, respectively, illustrate how these peer groupings inform planning.

Once again, rather than trying to ferret out the University's data in a comparative data table, the graphical representation conveys the information far more quickly and clearly. In looking at both Figures 8.4 and 8.5, it is evident that the University of

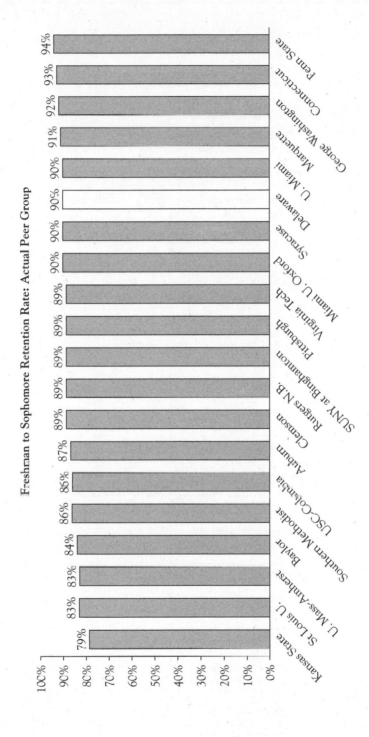

Freshman to Sophomore Retention Rate: Actual Peer Group

Penn State	94%
Connecticut	93%
George Washington	92%
Marquette	91%
U. Miami	90%
Delaware	90%
Syracuse	90%
Miami U. Oxford	90%
Virginia Tech	89%
Pittsburgh	89%
SUNY at Binghamton	89%
Rutgers N.B.	89%
Clemson	89%
Auburn	87%
USC-Columbia	85%
Southern Methodist	86%
Baylor	84%
U. Mass-Amherst	83%
St Louis U.	83%
Kansas State	79%

Figure 8.4 Peer Comparison of Freshman-to-Sophomore Retention Rates

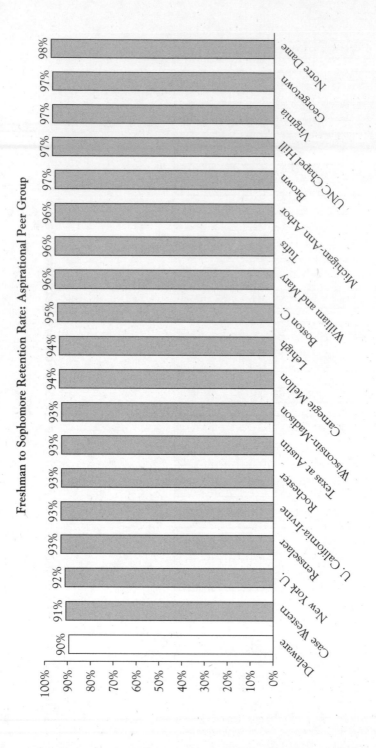

Freshman to Sophomore Retention Rate: Aspirational Peer Group

Delaware	90%
Case Western	91%
New York U.	92%
Rensselaer	93%
U. California-Irvine	93%
Rochester	93%
Texas at Austin	93%
Wisconsin-Madison	93%
Carnegie Mellon	94%
Lehigh	94%
Boston C.	95%
William and Mary	96%
Tufts	96%
Michigan-Ann Arbor	96%
Brown	97%
UNC Chapel Hill	97%
Virginia	97%
Georgetown	97%
Notre Dame	98%

Figure 8.4 (Continued)

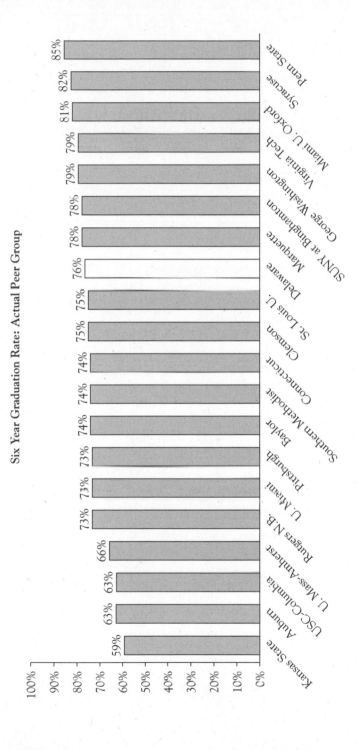

Six Year Graduation Rate: Actual Peer Group

Penn State	85%
Syracuse	82%
Miami U. Oxford	81%
Virginia Tech	79%
George Washington	79%
SUNY at Binghamton	78%
Marquette	78%
Delaware	76%
St. Louis U.	75%
Clemson	75%
Connecticut	74%
Southern Methodist	74%
Baylor	74%
U. Miami	73%
Pittsburgh	73%
Rutgers N.B.	73%
U. Mass-Amherst	66%
USC-Columbia	63%
Auburn	63%
Kansas State	59%

Figure 8.5 Peer Comparison of Six-Year Graduation Rates

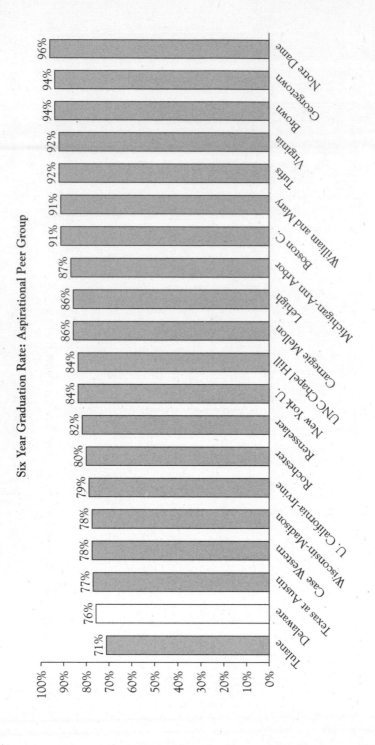

Six Year Graduation Rate: Aspirational Peer Group

Figure 8.5 (Continued)

Delaware is very favorably positioned among its actual peer institutions. But when inserted among aspirational peer universities, it is evident exactly what the University of Delaware needs to achieve with respect to retention and graduation to find a place within that grouping. The representations in Figures 8.4 and 8.5 are prototypes. At this writing, a Strategic Dashboard is under construction. Figure 8.6 displays the template for that dashboard. Each data box will display the University of Delaware value for the variable under examination, the high peer value, average peer value, and low peer value, and where the University value is relative to the average. When the user clicks on the University of Delaware value, a chart comparable to those in Figures 8.4 and 8.5 will appear. At the top of the dashboard are buttons that allow the user to view actual peers or aspirational peers. This is a highly effective and convenient means of conveying the University's relative position among actual and aspirational peers on key indicators of institutional effectiveness. It is a visual road map for what the institution must accomplish strategically if it wishes to move toward the aspirational group.

Dashboards are not only extremely useful for quickly communicating strategic information on key institutional performance indicators, but also relatively easy to build. There are a number of commercial vendors who provide basic software for building dashboards, but there is also a substantial amount of freeware available. The University of Delaware dashboards are constructed on a framework that was developed by Marywood University in Pennsylvania and presented at an annual meeting of the North East Association for Institutional Research, where the presenting institution offered to share it with the audience. Similar examples can be found by using any search engine, and the keywords "higher education dashboards."

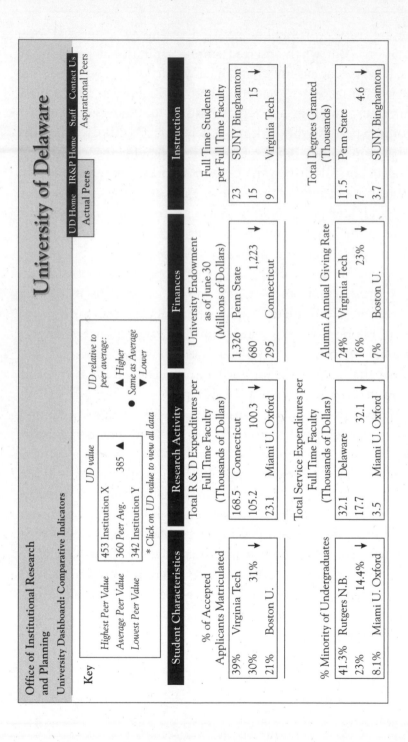

Figure 8.6 Template for University of Delaware Strategic Dashboard

Summary

The key to successful assessment of institutional effectiveness is to ensure that the information from those assessments is actually used to inform strategic planning, decision making, and resource allocation at a college or university. Information will actually be used only when it is readily assimilated and understood. Key decision makers at postsecondary institutions live in an environment of multitasking, and it is highly unlikely that they will devote a significant block of their time to deciphering long, detailed analytical assessment reports crowded with dense data tables and statistical descriptors. Conveying assessment information entails getting the central points across quickly and comprehensibly. That is most often done through concise executive summaries, using visual communication such as charts and graphs that instantly convey the central message. This chapter has focused on strategies for conveying information in just such a fashion, keeping the message simple, uncluttered, and, wherever possible, in pictorial form.

9

WHERE DO WE GO FROM HERE?

The first eight chapters of this book have concentrated on providing a broad, practical survey of strategies for assessing the various dimensions of institutional effectiveness. As noted in the preface, this volume was never intended to be a theoretical treatise in the underpinnings of assessment; rather, it was intended to identify the fundamental issues related to measuring institutional effectiveness, and to provide the reader with a basic understanding of how to approach those measurements. That said, there is sound theory that undergirds good assessment practice. If this volume has successfully whetted the reader's appetite for such theory, this closing chapter will provide some guideposts.

Student Engagement and Satisfaction

Chapter Three focused on strategies for assessing student behaviors as they relate to admissions, precollege determination of academic and social needs, student engagement and student satisfaction during the college years, and beyond. The relationship between student engagement and success was documented in Chapter Three in the writings of Astin (1985) and Pascarella and Terenzini (2005). However, for the reader of this book who is seeking a comprehensive and thoughtful synthesis of the research on factors that contribute to student success in college, the volume by Kuh, Kinzie, Buckley, Bridges, and Hayek (2007), "Piecing Together the Student Success Puzzle: Research, Propositions, and Recommendations," is a wonderfully compact and readable resource. In that volume, the authors provide an excellent framework for thinking about the various factors that impact student success, and have graphically represented it in Figure 9.1.

The authors devote the volume to a review of the literature on the variables depicted in Figure 9.1. Although certain external variables—such as economic forces, globalism, and state and federal policies—are to a large extent beyond an institution's control, even when accurately measured, Figure 9.1 also homes in on success factors that were described in Chapter Three as eminently measurable, and over which institutions *do* have influence. Precollege experiences include enrollment choices, which can be better understood through the admissions research activity described in Chapter

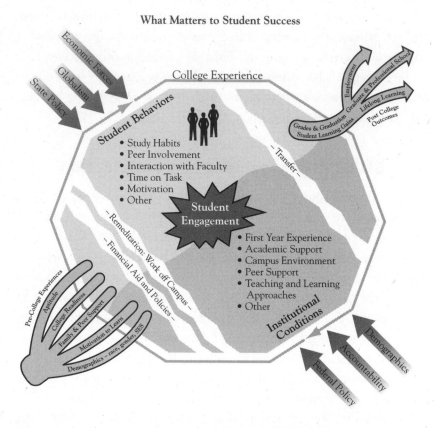

What Matters to Student Success

Figure 9.1 Forces Impacting Student Success

Source: Kuh, Kinzie, Buckley, Bridges, and Hayek (2007).

Three, using the Admitted Student Questionnaire or a comparable instrument. Academic preparation, aptitude, and college readiness can be directly or indirectly measured through strategies outlined in Chapter Three, which included the College Student Needs Assessment Survey or the College Student Expectations Questionnaire. Actual student behaviors that contribute to student success—study habits, interaction with faculty, time on task, and so on—are all measured within the National Survey of Student Engagement, of which Kuh and his colleagues are developers. Postgraduation outcomes are assessed through the sort of analysis seen at the end of Chapter Four with respect to alumni placement, and they are further enhanced by alumni research as described at the conclusion of Chapter Three. In short, the major factors affecting student engagement and student success are measurable, and strategies for such assessment were described in detail in Chapter Three. But as has been emphasized repeatedly, this book was written as a broad survey of how to approach the *practice* of assessing institutional effectiveness. The Kuh et al. (2007) volume is a wonderful summary of the *research* that underpins that practice. The volume also extends those research findings to describe specific recommendations and policies for enhancing college readiness, student engagement, and postgraduation outcomes, all of which are concretely applicable within institutional settings.

A second resource that bases much of its policy development and research on data from the National Survey of Student Engagement and on other activity from the Indiana University Center for Postsecondary Research is Kuh, Kinzie, Schuh, Whitt, and Associates (2005), *Student Success in College: Creating Conditions That Matter.* This volume summarizes the results of the Documenting Effective Educational Practice (DEEP) Project, which encompassed twenty colleges and universities across the United States that exemplify best practice in student success. The importance of this volume, which describes the institutional strategies for student success at each of the DEEP institutions, is that it effectively debunks the notion that good assessment can occur only at small colleges and universities with relatively small populations. The twenty institutions involved in the DEEP Project were:

Alverno College	University of Kansas
California State University – Monterey Bay	University of Maine – Farmington
The Evergreen State University	University of Michigan
Fayetteville State University	Sewanee: The University of the South
George Mason University	University of Texas at El Paso
Gonzaga University	Ursinus College
Longwood University	Wabash College
Macalester College	Wheaton College
Miami University	Winston-Salem State University
Sweet Briar College	Wofford College

Certainly the list includes Alverno, Macalester, and Wabash Colleges—small liberal arts institutions—but participants also included universities of significant complexity, such as Michigan, Kansas, George Mason, and Miami University. For the reader seeking institutional examples of best practice in assessing institutional effectiveness as it relates to student success, this volume is a must for the resource shelf. Kuh, Kinzie, Schuh, and Whitt (2005) wrote a companion piece, *Assessing Conditions to Enhance Institutional Effectiveness*, which draws on the lessons learned from the DEEP Project to create the Inventory for Student Engagement and Success (ISES) that provides an analytical framework for examining the institutional factors that lead to student success. Of particular importance is the extent to which ISES forces an institution to focus upon the six conditions and properties common to the best practice institutions in the DEEP Project:

- A "living" mission and a "lived" educational philosophy
- An unshakeable focus on student learning

- Environments adapted for educational enrichment
- Clear pathways to student success
- An improvement-oriented ethos
- Shared responsibility for educational quality and student success (Kuh, Kinzie, Schuh, and Whitt, 2005, 17)

The authors further argue that certain effective educational practices—all measurable through the National Survey of Student Engagement—will foster an environment in which those six conditions that nurture student success can flourish.

In short, the literature supports the proposition that student engagement and satisfaction contribute to retention and success; thus the strategies for measuring engagement and success described in Chapter Three are important. But also important are the lessons learned from the research of George Kuh and his colleagues at Indiana University on institutional best practices in student engagement and in fostering an institutional environment that leads to student success.

Measuring Student Learning

Chapter Four was intended to provide the reader with a broad overview of those strategies most commonly used to measure student learning in colleges and universities. As stated in Chapter Four, the discussion was a view of student learning outcomes assessment from thirty thousand feet—intended to be not an in-depth treatment, but rather a description of how learning outcomes assessment fits in with the overall assessment of institutional assessment. That said, the reader interested in more detailed information on measuring student learning is not without resources, several of which were cited in Chapter Four.

Actually engaging in meaningful and fruitful assessment of student learning outcomes requires activity at two levels—institutional and academic discipline. While one goal for any college or university ought to be the capability to demonstrate with multiple bodies of evidence that students in all of their disciplines are making measurable cognitive gains, the requirement, mandated by institutional and programmatic accrediting bodies, for multiple measures of student learning can be confounding, requiring different measures for different disciplines. As noted in Chapter Four, one would hope for a different set of strategies and measures for student learning in a Department of Philosophy than would be found in a Department of Chemical Engineering. Academic institutions and accreditors appreciate the complexity of measuring student learning within the disciplines, but that complexity is often lost on those outside of the academy. They assume, a priori, that students have mastered the content within their disciplines. Parents, employers, donors, legislators, and other interested parties are looking for evidence that students have mastered skills that will equip them for the world of work and for making meaningful contributions to society. In short, they are requiring students to be equipped with what we refer to as "general education" skills.

Mastery of general education used to be defined in terms of cross-disciplinary courses taken: that is, X number of credits in humanities, Y number in social sciences, Z number in natural and physical sciences, and so on. Throw in the mandatory requirement for courses such as foreign language and mathematics, and the student was certain to be well rounded at graduation. The problem was that completion of courses did not necessarily translate into demonstrable competencies. Colleges and universities have moved away from that notion to a model that typically defines general education in terms of measurable skills or competencies that all graduates of the institution are expected to demonstrate. Consider the following general education skills defined by the faculty at the University of Delaware:

Undergraduate Education at the University of Delaware aims to ensure that every student will:

1. Attain effective skills in oral and written communication, quantitative reasoning, and the use of information technology.

2. Learn to think critically to solve problems.

3. Be able to work and learn both independently and collaboratively.

4. Engage questions of ethics and recognize responsibilities to self, community, and society at large.

5. Understand the diverse ways of thinking that underlie the search for knowledge in the arts, humanities, sciences and social sciences.

6. Develop the intellectual curiosity, confidence, and engagement that will lead to lifelong learning.

7. Develop the ability to integrate academic knowledge with experiences that extend the boundaries of the classroom.

8. Expand understanding and appreciation of human creativity and diverse forms of aesthetic and intellectual expression.

9. Understand the foundations of United States society including the significance of its cultural diversity.

10. Develop an international perspective in order to live and work effectively in an increasingly global society. (University of Delaware Faculty Senate General Education Resolution, March 13, 2000: http://www.udel.edu/facsen/reports/genedrpt1.htm)

The Middle States Commission on Higher Education helps its member institutions to further distill the list of general education competencies to the following:

- consistent with institutional mission, a program of general education that incorporates study of values, ethics, and diverse perspectives;

- institutional requirements assuring that, upon degree completion, students are proficient in oral and written communication, scientific and quantitative reasoning, and technological competency appropriate to the discipline (Middle States Commission on Higher Education, 2006, 48)

The problem is how to measure these skills, at the institutional and discipline level. In Chapter Four, the argument was made that meta-experiences provide the best framework for measuring general education. By meta-experiences, we are referring to learning vehicles such as Freshman Year Experience (FYE), capstone experiences such as a senior thesis or undergraduate research project, or a student portfolio, either electronic or hardcopy. All of these meta-experiences compel students to draw on the full range of their educational experiences to demonstrate mastery of core general education competencies. For the reader interested in a broad range of examples of best practice in measuring general education competencies using approaches and strategies that are portable across institutions, see Marilee Bresciani's edited volume of case studies, *Assessing Student Learning in General Education: Good Practice Case Studies* (2007). The book contains illustrative case studies of exemplary assessment of general education in institutions ranging from community colleges (such as Paradise Valley Community College) to small, private colleges (such as Alverno College, Coker College) to complex universities (such as North Carolina State University, University of Cincinnati) to an entire university system—the State University of New York. It is a practical and highly readable volume of institutional illustrations of how to conceptualize general education at an institution, how to overcome faculty resistance and involve them as key proponents of general education measurement, and how to collect, interpret, and, most important, actually *use* general education assessments to improve learning and instruction—both institution-wide and within the disciplines—at a college or university.

Once the decision is made to move forward with assessment of general education, it is helpful to have a practical how-to manual to get the process off the ground. Readers will find that Barbara Walvoord's volume, *Assessment Clear and Simple: A Practical Guide for*

Institutions, Departments, and General Education (2004), falls into this category. The book assists the reader in identifying appropriate strategies for *direct* measurement of student learning (for example, tests, papers, class projects) as well as *indirect* measures (such as student and alumni surveys). It provides practical information on basic assessment tools such as writing course-embedded test items and writing rubrics for portfolio evaluation. It is brief, straightforward, and immensely usable.

Moving from general education to discipline-specific assessment of student learning outcomes and competencies, the reader is directed to Robert Diamond's comprehensive work, *Designing and Assessing Courses and Curricula: A Practical Guide* (2008). Written with a faculty audience in mind, this book empowers faculty with a central role in accreditation and accountability activity. It provides a solid grounding in the theory of assessment at the course and program level and guides faculty through the process of developing measurable learning goals; selecting the appropriate assessment instruments; individually, and collaboratively as faculty, measuring student learning along prescribed criteria; and actually using the assessments to improve instruction and learning. The volume is timely in addressing strategies for assessing student learning via distance education and web-based instruction. It speaks to the educational needs not only of traditional students but of adult learners as well. It provides faculty with a road map for developing a learning-centered syllabus, one that focuses on student achievement rather than faculty expectations (although the latter, when clearly articulated, drive the former). It is a marvelously rich and textured volume that should be on the resource shelf of anyone seriously interested in student learning as a key component of overall institutional effectiveness.

Measuring student learning is, indeed, central to describing the effective institution. Walvoord (2004) indicated that if she had to provide three institution-wide measures of institutional effectiveness, they would be

1. Retention and graduation rates.

2. A national student survey (note: the author of this volume would suggest something like the National Survey of Student Engagement).

3. "A very tight, manageable portfolio sample [of student work] evaluated by a large number of faculty, according to criteria that faculty have generated, to enhance faculty knowledge of the kinds of work that students are doing across the campus, and thus inform faculty teaching and deliberations about curriculum and pedagogy." (42)

The intent of this book, in Chapters Three and Four collectively, has been to enable the reader to meet and exceed Walvoord's three minimal measures of institutional effectiveness.

Costs and Productivity

Chapters Five, Six, and Seven examined the dimensions of institutional expenditures and productivity as components of institutional effectiveness. All three chapters outlined practical strategies for assessing those dimensions, and in so doing, focused less on the literature and more on the practice. The author of this book has been writing on cost and productivity for nearly two decades, and the reader interested in the evolution of work in that area—including its theoretical underpinnings—is directed to the Resources list of articles, chapters, and books for further reading, found at the end of this volume. Those writings not only trace the author's thought process in examining the issue of costs and productivity in higher education but also document the evolution of institutional effectiveness assessment strategies in this area over the course of two decades. Begun as an institutional effort to develop appropriate metrics for allocating internal resources at one institution (the budget support data described in Chapter Five), this movement has burgeoned into a full-blown, state-of-the-art data collection consortium (Delaware Study of Instructional Costs and Productivity) that is relied on by public and private four-year institutions across the United States, and which spawned a comparable two-year institution consortium (Kansas Study of Instructional Costs and Productivity). The importance of the Delaware Study as a tool for assessing institutional effectiveness was highlighted in a January 2009 discussion paper distributed by the National Association of State Universities and Land Grant Colleges (NASULGC) on the issue of tuitions and their relationship with cost (McPherson and Shulenburger, 2009). A thorough understanding of the evolution of these cost and productivity metrics underscores their utility in measuring academic components of institutional effectiveness.

With respect to administrative productivity, in addition to the Taylor and Massy volume *Strategic Indicators for Higher Education* (1996), referenced in Chapter Seven, the reader is directed to the following additional resources. Ratio analysis was highlighted as a useful tool for assessing institutional effectiveness through a financial lens. The topic is discussed in far greater detail in the highly readable and useful book *Strategic Financial Analysis for Higher Education*, sixth edition (Prager, Sealy & Co., LLC, KPMG LLP, and BearingPoint, Inc., 2005), available from the National Association of Collegiate and University Business Officers (www.nacubo. org). The book provides strong conceptual underpinnings for the various ratios used in financial analysis as well as specific examples of how to apply ratio analysis to all types of institutions, ranging from community colleges to small liberal arts institutions to complex research universities. It also addresses and largely resolves the differences in accounting standards between public and private institutions.

Finally, Robert Dickeson has written a book, *Prioritizing Academic Programs and Services: Reallocating Resources to Achieve Strategic Balance* (1999), that provides solid grounding in the criteria for program enhancement as well as program reduction or elimination. One of the more difficult decisions in higher education is the determination that a program must lose significant resources and, in some instances, be retrenched. The Dickeson book focuses on the centrality of programs to the institutional mission and provides a clear framework for assessing the extent to which programs contribute to the fulfillment of that mission.

Some Final Words

This book was written primarily to help colleges and universities assess the effectiveness of their academic and nonacademic operations and the extent to which they are meeting the needs of mission-defined and mission-driven markets. Much of the discussion regarding the effectiveness of higher education institutions centers on the capacity of those institutions to demonstrate that students are, indeed, learning and are graduating having demonstrably acquired both discipline-specific and general education competencies that were clearly articulated and systematically measured throughout those students' academic career. Equally important is the capacity to measure the effectiveness and efficiency of the deployment of human and fiscal resources in support of student learning and other central facets of the institutional mission. This book was written to provide institutions with strategies for reaching a fundamentally better understanding of the institution's effectiveness. A secondary, but important by-product of this introspection and self-assessment is the capacity to better communicate with accrediting bodies—both institutional and programmatic—about the institution's compliance with stated accreditation standards. In that regard, the reader is encouraged to explore the works of Edward Tufte of Yale University, who has written extensively on visual communication. His work is cited in the list of Resources for further reading at the end of this volume.

When first conceptualizing this volume, the author gave serious consideration to delving into the issue of public accountability. After careful thought, the decision was made not to go that route. Extensive reading in the area of public accountability in higher education made it apparent that colleges and universities require greater precision in what they measure, how the information is interpreted, and how it is best communicated. The accountability movement, best described in Burke and Associates' book *Achieving Accountability in Higher Education* (2005), describes the interplay between the higher education community and external forces that include state and federal government and the marketplace—defined as those who consume the products of higher education, be it graduates, pure or applied research, or other forms of intellectual capital. Burke's book describes the inherent tension between those inside the academy and external forces demanding greater transparency from postsecondary institutions. To be sure, politics and other social forces contribute to this tension. But much of that tension is also the result of imperfect communication among the parties.

Ultimately, this book was written to help us achieve that greater precision in assessing and talking about institutional effectiveness. Aside from talking to our colleagues within our institutions about how assessments can better inform institutional decisions related to continuous improvement, the book was intended to help shape the language that we use to talk with external accreditors about how effectively our colleges and universities perform. The more we master both the practice of and conversation about the assessment of institutional effectiveness and its relationship to solid strategic planning with our institutions and accreditors, the better prepared we will be to extend that conversation to those outside of higher education. It is the author's intention that this book, in some measure, contribute to the evolution of that conversation.

APPENDIX A

UNIVERSITY OF DELAWARE COLLEGE SELECTION SURVEY

Part One: General Information

INSTRUCTIONS: For each item below, please circle the number of your response or answer the question by writing your response. For example, if you are female, circle number 2 in the first question below.

1. Sex
   1. Male
   2. Female
2. Home State: _____ (e.g. DE, NJ, PA, NY, etc.)
3. (a) From what type of high school did you graduate?
       1. Public
       2. Private
       3. Parochial
   (b) State where the high school is located: _____
4. Race/ethnic group:
   1. American Indian
   2. Asian/Pacific Islander
   3. Black
   4. Hispanic
   5. White
   6. Other

5. Please indicate your cumulative high school GPA:
   1. 3.5 or higher
   2. 3.0–3.49
   3. 2.5–2.99
   4. 2.0–2.49
   5. 2.0 or lower

6. Please indicate your highest SAT score:

   SATV ___
   SATM ___
   SATW ___

7. Into which College at the University of Delaware were you accepted?
   1. Agriculture
   2. Arts & Science (except undeclared)
   3. Arts & Science, undeclared
   4. Business & Economics
   5. Education
   6. Engineering
   7. Human Resources
   8. Nursing
   9. Physical Education

8. To how many colleges or universities did you apply?
   1. One
   2. Two
   3. Three
   4. Four
   5. Five
   6. Six
   7. Seven or more

Part Two: College Selection

1. Please list in order of preference the three colleges or university that were at the top of your application list. Then answer the two questions to the right.

	Were You Accepted?		Were You Awarded Any Financial Aid?		
1st choice ___	Yes	No	Yes	No	Did not apply for aid
2nd choice ___	1	2	1	2	3
3rd choice ___	1	2	1	2	3

2. During the college choice process, did your preference for the University of Delaware change?

   1. Yes, moved up

   2. Yes, moved down

   3. Did not change

3. (a) Were you offered a scholarship strictly based on academic merit from the University of Delaware?

      1. Yes

      2. No

   (b) Were you offered a scholarship strictly based on academic merit from other schools?

      1. Yes

      2. No

         If yes, please name the other schools:_____

   (c) If you did receive a scholarship based strictly on academic merit, was it the decisive factor in your final college choice?

      1. Yes

      2. No

4. Which of the following statements best characterizes your college enrollment decision?

1. I am enrolled at the University of Delaware.

2. I am enrolled at another college. (Please specify: _____)

3. I am uncertain where I will be enrolling.

4. I am not enrolling at any college at this time.

Part Three: College-University Characteristics

We want to learn about how you view the characteristics of the University of Delaware in comparison to other colleges and universities to which you have applied, been accepted, and seriously considered attending. Please complete this section by first indicating how important the characteristic was in influencing your enrollment decision (circle the most appropriate response). **If you are attending Delaware next fall,** indicate how you rate the various characteristics at both the University of Delaware and the school you would have selected had you not decided to enroll at Delaware. **Be sure to write the name** of the school you would have attended in the blank provided. **If you are attending a different college,** indicate how Delaware compares to the school you will be attending. Again, **be sure to include the name** of the school you will be attending. If you do not know enough about an item, please indicate "don't know" (circle number 5).

Of the characteristics above, which three factors (in order of importance) most influenced your enrollment decision?

Most important factor: ___ Second most important: ___ Third most important: ___

Part Three: College-University Characteristics

Characteristics	How Important Is This to You?			University of Delaware					School You Would Have or Will Attend			
	Very Important	Somewhat Important	Not Important	Very Good	Good	Poor	Very Poor	Don't Know	Very Good	Good	Poor	Don't Know
1. Quality of academics	1	2	3	1	2	3	4	5	1	2	3	4
2. Honors program	1	2	3	1	2	3	4	5	1	2	3	4
3. Personal attention given to students by faculty	1	2	3	1	2	3	4	5	1	2	3	4
4. General reputation of university	1	2	3	1	2	3	4	5	1	2	3	4
5. Quality of faculty	1	2	3	1	2	3	4	5	1	2	3	4
6. Total cost (tuition, fees, room/board)	1	2	3	1	2	3	4	5	1	2	3	4
7. Social activities	1	2	3	1	2	3	4	5	1	2	3	4
8. Financial aid package	1	2	3	1	2	3	4	5	1	2	3	4

(continued)

Part Three: College-University Characteristics (continued)

	How Important Is This to You?			University of Delaware					School You Would Have or Will Attend			
	Very Important	Somewhat Important	Not Important	Very Good	Good	Poor	Very Poor	Don't Know	Very Good	Good	Poor	Don't Know
9. Quality of programs in your intended major												
10. Diversity of student body	1	2	3	1	2	3	4	5	1	2	3	4
11. Intercollegiate programs	1	2	3	1	2	3	4	5	1	2	3	4
12. Housing opportunities	1	2	3	1	2	3	4	5	1	2	3	4
13. Athletic facilities	1	2	3	1	2	3	4	5	1	2	3	4
14. Faculty teaching reputation	1	2	3	1	2	3	4	5	1	2	3	4
15. Closeness to home	1	2	3	1	2	3	4	5	1	2	3	4
16. Size of enrollment	1	2	3	1	2	3	4	5	1	2	3	4
17. Overall treatment as prospective student	1	2	3	1	2	3	4	5	1	2	3	4
18. Promptness of replies to requests for information	1	2	3	1	2	3	4	5	1	2	3	4

Part Four: Information Sources

We are interested in learning which sources of information students use to learn about the University of Delaware, whether the information provided by the source was positive or negative, and how important that source and information was in shaping your choice of a college. For each of the information sources **that you actually used**, please indicate whether the information you received about the University was positive or negative. Also, for those sources you used, indicate how important that information was to you in your selection of a college. Circle the number corresponding to your choice.

List in order of importance (by selecting from the numbers 1–15, above) the three most important influences on your decision as to which college to attend:

Most important influence: ___ Second most important:___ Third most important: ___

Thank you for your cooperation.

Part Four: Information Sources

Information Source	Impact						Importance		
	Didn't use this resource	Very Positive	Positive	No Impact	Negative	Very Important	Very Important	Somewhat Important	Not Important
1. Viewbook	1	2	3	4	5	6	1	2	3
2. Campus visit	1	2	3	4	5	6	1	2	3
3. Catalog	1	2	3	4	5	6	1	2	3
4. College comparison guides (Peterson's, Baron's)	1	2	3	4	5	6	1	2	3
5. Parents	1	2	3	4	5	6	1	2	3
6. Friends	1	2	3	4	5	6	1	2	3
7. Current students	1	2	3	4	5	6	1	2	3
8. High school teacher	1	2	3	4	5	6	1	2	3
9. High school guidance teacher	1	2	3	4	5	6	1	2	3
10. Alumnus	1	2	3	4	5	6	1	2	3
11. High school visit by faculty member	1	2	3	4	5	6	1	2	3
12. Mailing from the Honors Program	1	2	3	4	5	6	1	2	3
13. High school visit by admissions officer	1	2	3	4	5	6	1	2	3
14. Athletic staff	1	2	3	4	5	6	1	2	3
15. Home/hotel reception	1	2	3	4	5	6	1	2	3

APPENDIX B

UNIVERSITY OF DELAWARE 2007 STUDY OF INSTRUCTION COSTS AND PRODUCTIVITY, BY ACADEMIC DISCIPLINE

NOTE: As you read the definitions and calculations referred to below, you should examine the copy of the data collection form also found on this packet.

Definitions of Terms

Academic Department/Discipline: The disciplines selected for benchmarking in this study are found in the "Classification of Instructional Programs" taxonomy, which is derived directly from the National Center for Education Statistics' CIP Code system. Wherever possible, we are benchmarking data at the four-digit CIP code level. That is, we will be looking at discrete disciplines within a broad curricular field. (See note below.) For example, in Engineering, CIP Code 14.XX, you will be asked to provide data for those engineering disciplines at your institution. Suppose you had five engineering departments—agricultural, chemical, civil, electrical, and mechanical. You would provide data for five discrete CIP Codes, i.e., 14.03 (Agricultural Engineering), 14.07 (Chemical Engineering), 14.08 (Civil Engineering), 14.10 (Electrical Engineering), 14.19 (Mechanical Engineering). Institutions with different engineering departments would report data for the appropriate four-digit engineering CIP codes. The pattern would be repeated across other curricular areas. If you have difficulty disaggregating categories within a specific disciplinary area, there is a general CIP code, typically XX.01, that should be used. For example, if your Department of Foreign Languages offers French, Spanish, Russian, Chinese, Greek, and Latin, and you cannot cleanly disaggregate teaching workload and cost data into each of these disciplines, simply report the data as "Foreign Languages and Literature," CIP Code 16.01. If a disciplinary area provides no "general" option, and you cannot cleanly disaggregate to specific curricular area, report a two-digit CIP code, e.g. Engineering-Related Technologies would be 15.00.

NOTE: Members of the Southern Universities Group and a number of other institutions have asked to benchmark at the six-digit CIP level. All participating institutions are encouraged to provide six-digit CIP codes in as many instances as feasible, and we will benchmark at that level wherever possible. Those data will then be rolled up to the four-digit level, at which all institutions will be benchmarked, consistent with the discussion above.

Degree Offerings: Please indicate all of the degrees, i.e., bachelors, masters, doctorate, offered in this discipline at your institution. In the space next to each of the degrees, we ask that you provide the average number of degrees awarded in the discipline for each of the past three academic years (2004–05, 2005–06, 2006–07) as reported to IPEDS. We will again benchmark, in a separate section of the report, the data based upon highest degree offered.

Part A: Instructional Workload—Fall 2006 Semester

NOTE: The following discussion of faculty should be read within the context of your institution's Fall 2006 census data.

THE DUE DATE FOR SUBMISSION OF DATA IS JANUARY 28, 2009.

Regular Faculty: Regular faculty are defined as those individuals who are hired for the purpose of doing teaching, and who may also do research and/or service. They are characterized by a recurring contractual relationship in which the individual and the institution both assume a continuing appointment. These faculty typically fall into two categories:

Tenured and Tenure-Eligible: Those individuals who either hold tenure, or for whom tenure is an expected outcome. At most institutions, these are full, associate, and assistant professors.

Non-Tenure Track Faculty: Those individuals who teach on a recurring contractual basis, but whose academic title renders them ineligible for academic tenure. At most institutions, these titles include instructors, lecturers, visiting faculty, etc.

Supplemental Faculty: Supplemental faculty are characteristically paid to teach out of a pool of temporary funds. Their appointment is non-recurring, although the same individual might receive a temporary appointment in successive terms. The key point is that the funding is, by nature, temporary and there is no expectation of continuing appointment. This category includes adjuncts, administrators or professional personnel at the institution who teach but whose primary job responsibility is non-faculty, contributed service personnel, etc..

Teaching Assistants: Students at the institution who receive a stipend strictly for teaching activity. Includes teaching assistants who are instructors of record, but also includes teaching assistants who function as discussion section leaders, laboratory section leaders, and other types of organized class sections in which instruction takes place but which may not carry credit and for which there is no formal instructor of record. For purposes of this study, do not include graduate research assistants.

In calculating full time equivalency (FTE Faculty) for each of the faculty categories described above, the following conventions are recommended:

REGULAR FACULTY: Take the TOTAL FTE for filled faculty positions as they appear in the Fall 2006 personnel file at your institution, and report this in the "Total FTE Faculty" data field. (Column A) Be sure to report filled positions only. Filled positions are those that have salaries associated with them. Include paid leaves such as sabbaticals wherein the individual is receiving a salary, but exclude unpaid leaves of absence. In Column B, report the FTE portion of faculty lines that are supported by external or separately budgeted funds for purposes other than teaching, i.e., research or service. The remainder is the departmental or program instructional faculty FTE, and should be reported in the "Instructional" FTE faculty data field. That is, the FTE for Column C is computed by subtracting Column B from Column A. For example, suppose Professor Jones is a full time member of the Chemistry Faculty. He would be reflected as 1.0 FTE in Column A. Professor Jones has a research grant that contractually obligates him to spend one-third of his time in research. The externally supported portion of his position is 0.33 FTE, which would be reflected in Column B. As a result, 0.66 FTE is the instructional faculty which would appear in Column C, i.e., 1.0 FTE (Column A) minus 0.33 FTE (Column B).

SUPPLEMENTAL FACULTY: Full time equivalency for supplemental faculty can be arrived at by taking the total teaching credit hours (which are generally equivalent to the credit value of the course(s) taught) for each supplemental faculty, and dividing by 12. Twelve hours is a broadly accepted standard for a full time teaching load. (If your institution assigns one course unit instead of three or four credit hours to a course being taught, use a divisor of 4). Because Supplemental Faculty generally are not generally supported by external funds, Column C will typically equal Column A.

TEACHING ASSISTANTS: You are asked to assign an FTE value to teaching assistants, apportioned between credit bearing course activity where the teaching assistant is the instructor of record, and non-credit bearing course activity (i.e., section leader for zero-credit laboratories, discussion sections, recitation sections). To do this, take the FTE value for teaching assistants in a given academic department or program, as it appears in your personnel file. Then apportion the FTE as follows:

Credit Bearing Courses: Use the same convention as with Supplemental Faculty. Take all courses which are credit bearing and for which teaching assistants are the instructors of record, and divide the total teaching credit hours by 12. The resulting quotient is the teaching assistant FTE for credit bearing course activity.

Non-Credit Bearing Activity: From the total teaching assistant FTE, taken from your personnel file, subtract the calculated FTE for credit bearing activity as outlined above. The difference is the FTE for non-credit bearing activity. It is understood that on many campuses, the non-credit bearing activity is not exclusively instructional, and may include activities such as grading papers. However, the decision to allow teaching assistants to do things other than teach is analogous to allowing other departmentally paid faculty types to take reduced loads to engage in non-teaching activity. In both instances, salaries are associated with personnel, and in the interest of consistency, the personnel should be counted as a component of common practice in higher education.

NOTE: In looking at student credit hours generated, by level of instruction, and number of organized class sections taught, refer only to your institution's Fall 2006 semester workload file. Do not report data here for the full academic year.

Course: An instructional activity, identified by academic discipline and number, in which students enroll, typically to earn academic credit applicable to a degree objective. Excludes "non-credit courses," but includes "zero credit course sections" which are requirements of or prerequisites to degree programs, and which are scheduled, and consume institutional or departmental resources in the same manner as "credit courses." Zero-credit course sections are typically supplements to the credit-bearing lecture portion of a course. Zero credit sections are frequently listed as laboratory, discussion, or recitation sections in conjunction with the credit bearing lecture portion of a course.

Organized Class Course: A course which is provided principally by means of regularly scheduled classes meeting in classrooms or similar facilities at stated times.

Individual Instruction Course: A course in which instruction is not conducted in regularly scheduled class meetings. Includes "readings" or "special topics" courses, "problems" or "research" courses, including dissertation/thesis research, and "individual lesson" courses (typically in music and fine arts).

Course Section: A unique group of students which meets with one or more instructors.

In reporting the number of sections taught at the respective levels of instruction, to the extent that your database allows, please make certain **not** to double count dual listed (undergraduate and graduate sections of a single course meeting concurrently) and cross listed (a single course in which students from two or more disciplines may register under their respective department call letters) courses.

Course Credit: The academic credit value of a course; the value recorded for a student who successfully completes the course.

Lower Division Instruction: Courses typically associated with the first and second year of college study.

Upper Division Instruction: Courses typically associated with the third and fourth year of college study.

Graduate Level Instruction: Courses typically associated with post-baccalaureate study.

Student Credit Hours: The credit value of a course (typically 3 or 4 credits) multiplied by the enrollment in the course.

Student credit hours should be aggregated and reported on the data form on the basis of course level of instruction and the classification of the faculty member. It is important to underscore that the criterion is level of course as opposed to level of the student registered in the course. For example, the student credit hours generated by a second semester senior taking an introductory graduate course would be reported in the "graduate" column. Similarly, those generated by a first semester graduate student taking an upper division level prerequisite undergraduate course would be reported in the "upper division" column. (If your institution assigns one credit unit instead of three or four credit hours to a course, convert the units to credit hours by multiplying by 3 or 4, as appropriate.)

For institutions with doctoral level instruction, in the box below the Total for "Individual Instruction Graduate Student Credit Hours," please indicate the number of student credit hours from that Total that are devoted to dissertation supervision.

If you cannot differentiate between "Organized Class" and "Individualized Instruction" student credit hours, assign all credit hours to the appropriate "Organized Class" column. Similarly, if you cannot differentiate between "Lower Division" and "Upper Division" undergraduate student credit hours, report all those credit hours under "Total Undergraduate Credit Hours."

In addition to aggregation by course level, student credit hours should also be aggregated and reported, based upon the classification of the instructors teaching the respective courses. Student credit hours should be reported for all courses taught by a faculty member who is budgeted to a given department, regardless of whether the course is taught in that department or elsewhere. For example, a faculty member who is budgeted to the History Department, and whose teaching load includes two History courses and one Political Science course, should have all of the student credit hour generated from these courses credited to the History Department.

To the extent possible, deal with team teaching situations by prorating student credit hours to individual faculty in an appropriate fashion. If two faculty members are equally sharing instructional responsibilities for a 3 credit course with 30 students enrolled (90 student credit hours), 45 credit hours would be apportioned to Faculty A, and 45 credit hours to Faculty B. The same allocation would hold in appropriating the organized class section to the two faculty, i.e., 0.5 section to each. This is especially important where the faculty members in a team teaching situation are budgeted to different departments. The student credit hours should follow the faculty member. Use your institutional convention in making these prorating decisions.

The same conventions apply to reporting counts of organized class sections. The first column asks for the number of lab/discussion/recitation sections taught by each type of faculty. The remainder of the grid looks at all other organized class sections, disaggregated by level of instruction and by faculty type.

The foregoing data collection discussion refers to the **FALL 2006** *term. All institutions are expected to submit data for Fall 2006. Reminder: Due date for submission of data is January 28, 2009.*

Part B: Cost and Productivity Information

NOTE: The data collected on this portion of the data form require financial information for all of Fiscal Year 2007, and student credit hour data for the major terms in Academic Year 2006–07 which are supported by an academic department's basic operating budget. These major terms are generally Fall and Spring at institutions on a semester calendar, and Fall, Winter and Spring at institutions on a quarter calendar.

DUE DATE FOR SUBMISSION OF DATA IS JANUARY 28, 2009.

Student Credit Hour Data: You are asked to provide the total number of student credit hours taught at the undergraduate and graduate levels, respectively, during the 2006–07 academic year. "2006–07 Academic Year" refers only to those terms that are funded by the department's instructional budget. At most semester calendar institutions, this refers to the Fall and Spring terms; at quarter calendar institutions, Fall, Winter, and Spring terms are generally included. If instructional activity in a given term is funded by a source other than the departmental instructional budget (e.g., if the Summer term teaching is funded by the Special Sessions Office or Continuing Education, etc.), student credit hours associated with that term are to be excluded.

Direct Expenditure Data: This study asks for total direct expenditure data in certain functional areas—instruction, research, and public service. Direct expenditure data reflect costs incurred for personnel compensation, supplies, and services used in the conduct of each of these functional areas. They include acquisition costs of capital assets such as equipment and library books to the extent that funds are budgeted for and used by operating departments for instruction, research, and public service. For purposes of this report, exclude centrally allocated computing costs and centrally supported computer labs, and graduate student tuition remission and fee waivers.

Instruction: The instruction function, for purposes of this study, includes general academic instruction, occupational and vocational instruction, community education, preparatory and adult basic education, and remedial and tutorial instruction conducted by the teaching faculty for the institution's students. Departmental research and service **which are not separately budgeted** should be included under instruction. In other words, department research which is externally funded should be *excluded* from instructional expenditures, as should any departmental funds which were expended for the purpose of matching external research funds as part of a contractual or grant obligation. EXCLUDE expenditures for academic administration where the primary function is administration. For example, exclude deans, but include department chairs.

You are asked to disaggregate total instructional expenditures for each discipline into three pieces of data:

1. *Salaries*: Report all wages paid to support the instructional function in a given department or program during Fiscal Year 2000. While these will largely be faculty salaries, be sure to include clerical (e.g., department secretary), professionals (e.g., lab technicians), Graduate student stipends (but not tuition waivers), and any other personnel who support the teaching function and whose salaries and wages are paid **from the department's/program's instructional budget.**

2. *Benefits*: Report expenditures for benefits associated with the personnel for whom salaries and wages were reported on the previous entry. If you cannot separate benefits from salaries, but benefits are included in the salary figure you have entered, indicate "Included in Salaries" in the data field. Some institutions book benefits centrally and do not disaggregate to the department level. If you can compute the appropriate benefit amount for the department/program, please do so and enter the data. If you cannot do so, enter "NA" in the field, and we will impute a cost factor based upon the 2006–07 benefit rate for your institution, as published in *Academe*. If no rate is available, we will use a default value of 28%.

3. *Other Than Personnel Costs*: This category includes non-personnel items such as travel, supplies and expense, non-capital equipment purchases, etc., that are typically part of a department or program's cost of doing business. *Excluded* from this category are items such as central computing costs, centrally allocated computing labs, graduate student tuition remission and fee waivers, etc.

Research: This category includes all funds expended for activities specifically organized to produce research outcomes and commissioned by an agency either external to the institution or **separately budgeted** by an organizational unit within the institution. Report total research expenditures only. It is not necessary to disaggregate costs for this category.

Public Service: Report all funds **separately budgeted** specifically for public service and expended for activities established primarily to provide non-instructional services beneficial to groups external to the institution. Examples include cooperative extension and community outreach projects. Report total service expenditures only. It is not necessary to disaggregate costs for this category.

Respondents at institutions with interdisciplinary research and service "Centers" should make every attempt to disaggregate expenditures in those centers on a pro rata basis to component disciplines/departments. For those institutions with separate foundations for handling external research and service contracts and grants, funds processed by those foundations to departments/disciplines should be included.

References

A Test of Leadership: Charting the Future of U.S Higher Education. A Report of the Commission Appointed by Secretary of Education Margaret Spellings. Washington, D.C.: U.S. Department of Education, 2006.

Accrediting Commission for Senior Colleges and Universities. *Handbook of Accreditation.* Alameda, CA: Western Association of Colleges and Schools, 2001.

Astin, A. *Achieving Educational Excellence: A Critical Assessment of Priorities and Practices in Higher Education.* San Francisco: Jossey-Bass, 1985.

Boyer, E. L. *Scholarship Reconsidered: Priorities of the Professoriate.* Princeton, NJ: Carnegie Foundation for the Advancement of Teaching, 1990.

Boyer Commission on Educating Undergraduates in the Research University. *Reinventing Undergraduate Education.* Stony Brook, NY: State University of New York at Stony Brook, 1998.

Bresciani, M. J. (Ed.). *Assessing Student Learning in General Education: Good Practice Case Studies.* Bolton, MA: Anker Publishing, 2007.

Burke, J. C., and Associates. *Achieving Accountability in Higher Education: Balancing Public, Academic, and Market Demands.* San Francisco: Jossey-Bass, 2005.

Commission on Colleges. *The Principles of Accreditation: Foundations for Quality Enhancement.* Decatur, GA: Southern Association of Colleges and Schools, 2007.

Diamond, R. M. *Designing and Assessing Courses and Curricula: A Practical Guide,* 3rd ed. San Francisco: Jossey-Bass, 2008.

Dickeson R. *Prioritizing Academic Programs and Services: Reallocating Resources to Achieve Strategic Balance.* San Francisco: Jossey-Bass, 1999.

Dressel, P. "Grades: One More Tilt at the Windmill." Bulletin, Memphis State University, Center for the Study of Higher Education, 1976.

Harker, P. T. *The Path to Prominence.* University of Delaware, 2008.

Hollowell, D., M. F. Middaugh, and E. Sibolski. *Integrating Higher Education Planning and Assessment: A Practical Guide.* Ann Arbor, MI: Society for College and University Planning, 2006.

Kuh, G. D., J. Kinzie, J. A. Buckley, B. K. Bridges, and J. C. Hayek. "Piecing Together the Student Success Puzzle: Research, Propositions, and

Recommendations." *ASHE Higher Education Report* 32, no. 5. San Francisco: Jossey-Bass, 2007.

Kuh, G. D., J. Kinzie, J. H. Schuh, and E. J. Whitt. *Assessing Conditions to Enhance Educational Effectiveness: The Inventory for Student Engagement and Success.* San Francisco: Jossey-Bass, 2005.

Kuh, G. D., J. Kinzie, J. H. Schuh, E. J. Whitt, and Associates. *Student Success in College: Creating Conditions That Matter.* San Francisco: Jossey-Bass, 2005.

McPherson, P., and D. Shulenburger. *University Tuition, Consumer Choice, and College Affordability: Strategies for Addressing a Higher Education Affordability Challenge.* A NASULGC Discussion Paper. Washington, D.C.: Office of Public Affairs, National Association of State Universities and Land Grant Colleges, 2009. [http://www.nasulgc.org/NetCommunity/Page.aspx?pid=1088&srcid=183].

Middaugh, M. F. *Understanding Faculty Productivity: Standards and Benchmarks for Colleges and Universities.* San Francisco: Jossey-Bass, 2001.

Middaugh, M. F., R. Graham, and A. Shahid. *A Study of Higher Education Instructional Expenditures: The Delaware Study of Instructional Costs and Productivity (NCES 2003-161).* Washington, DC: U.S. Department of Education/National Center for Education Statistics, 2003.

Middle States Commission on Higher Education. *Middle States Evaluation Team Report,* 2001.

Middle States Commission on Higher Education. *Characteristics of Excellence: Eligibility Requirements and Standards for Accreditation.* Philadelphia, PA: Middle States Association of Colleges and Schools, 2006.

National Association of State Universities and Land Grant Colleges (NASULGC). Discussion paper, Jan. 2009. [http://www.nasulgc.org/NetCommunity/Page.aspx?pid=1088&srcid=183].

National Commission on the Cost of Higher Education. *Straight Talk About College Costs and Prices: Report of the National Commission on the Cost of Higher Education.* Phoenix.: Oryx Press, 1998.

New England Commission on Institutions of Higher Education. *Standards for Accreditation.* Bedford, MA: New England Association of Colleges and Schools, 2005.

North Central Higher Learning Commission. *Institutional Accreditation: An Overview,* 2007.

Northwest Commission on Colleges and Universities. *Accreditation Handbook.* Redmond, WA: Northwest Commission on Colleges and Universities, 2003.

Palomba, C. A., T. W. Banta, and Associates. *Assessment Essentials: Planning, Implementing, Improving.* San Francisco: Jossey-Bass, 1999.

Pascarella, E. T., and P. T. Terenzini. *How College Affects Students.* San Francisco: Jossey-Bass, 1991.

Pascarella, E. T., and P. T. Terenzini. *How College Affects Students: A Third Decade of Research*. San Francisco: Jossey-Bass, 2005.

Prager, Sealy & Co., LLC, KPMG LLP, and BearingPoint, Inc. *Strategic Financial Analysis for Higher Education*, 6th ed. Washington, DC: National Association of College and University Business Officers, 2005.

Southern Commission on Colleges. *The Principles of Accreditation: Foundations for Quality Enhancement*, 2007.

Spellings Commission. *A Test of Leadership: Charting the Future of U.S. Higher Education*. The Report of the Secretary's Commission on the Future of Higher Education, 2006 p. 4.

Suskie, L. A. *Assessing Student Learning: A Common Sense Guide*, 2nd ed. San Francisco: Wiley, 2009.

Taylor, B. E., and W. F. Massy. *Strategic Indicators for Higher Education: Vital Benchmarks and Information to Help You Evaluate and Improve Your Institution's Performance*. Princeton, NJ: Peterson's, 1996.

The Higher Learning Commission. *Institutional Accreditation: An Overview*. Chicago: North Central Association of Colleges and Schools, 2007.

University of Delaware. Faculty Senate General Education Resolution. March 13, 2000. http://www.udel.edu/facsen/reports/genedrpt1.htm.

University of Delaware. *Middle States Self-Study Report*, April 2001.

U.S. News and World Report. "America's Best Colleges, 1996." September 19, 1996.

Walvoord, B. E. *Assessment Clear and Simple: A Practical Guide for Institutions, Departments, and General Education*. San Francisco: Jossey-Bass, 2004.

Western Association of Colleges and Schools. *Handbook of Accreditation*, 2001.

Zemsky, R., and W. Massy. "Cost Containment: Committing to a New Economic Reality." *Change* 22, no. 6 (1990): 16–22

Web-Based References

Note: All website references cited were current at the time of writing.

ACT Evaluation Survey Services: http://www.act.org/ess/

American Association of State Colleges and Universities: www.aascu.org

American University, Office of Institutional Research and Assessment: http:// www.american.edu/academic.depts/provost/oir/assessment.html

Association of American Colleges and Universities: www.aacu.org

Brookdale Community College, Academic Assessment: http://www.brookdale. cc.nj.us/pages/388.asp

College Board, "ASQ and ASQ-Plus": http://professionals.collegeboard.com/ higher-ed/recruitment/asq

College Student Experiences Questionnaire: http://cseq.iub.edu/

CUPA-HR: http://www.cupahr.org/

Delaware Study of Faculty Activity: http://www.udel.edu/IR/focs/

Delaware Study of Instructional Costs and Productivity: www.udel.edu/ir/cost

Delaware Technical and Community College, "Future Students": http://www .dtcc.edu/future/

Delaware Technical and Community College, "Mission Statement": http://www .dtcc.edu/effectiveness/pages/mission_statement.html

Higher Education Research Institute, "Faculty Survey": http://www.gseis.ucla. edu/heri/facOverview.php

Integrated Postsecondary Educational Data System (IPEDS), "Executive Peer Tool and Peer Analysis System": http://nces.ed.gov/ipedspas/

Integrated Postsecondary Educational Data System (IPEDS), "Peer Analysis Tool": http://nces.ed.gov/ipedspas/mainScreen.asp

Kansas Study of Instructional Costs and Productivity: http://www.kansasstudy. org/

London Metropolitan University, Metranet: https://intranet.londonmet.ac.uk/

National Association of College and University Business Officers: www.nacubo .org

National Association of State Universities and Land Grant Colleges (NASULGC): www.nasulgc.org

National Association of State Universities and Land Grant Colleges, "University Tuition, Consumer Choice, and College Affordability": http://www.nasulgc.org/NetCommunity/Page.aspx?pid=1088&srcid=183

National Center for Education Statistics, "Fast Facts": http://nces.ed.gov/fast facts/display.asp?id=98

National Center for Education Statistics, "The College Navigator": http://nces.ed.gov/collegenavigator/

National Community College Benchmarking Project: http://www.nccbp.org/

National Study of Postsecondary Faculty: http://nces.ed.gov/surveys/nsopf/

National Survey of Student Engagement: http://nsse.iub.edu/index.cfm

National Survey of Student Engagement, "Developing Effective Educational Practices (DEEP) Project": http://nsse.iub.edu/institute/index.cfm?view=deep/overview

Noel Levitz Student Satisfaction Inventory: https://www.noellevitz.com/Our+Services/Retention/Tools/Student+Satisfaction+Inventory/

Society for College and University Planning: www.scup.org

Universidad Mayor, Santiago, Chile: http://www.umayor.cl/2008/

University of Delaware, Office of Educational Assessment: http://assessment.udel.edu/

University of Delaware Faculty Senate, "General Education Program": http://www.udel.edu/facsen/reports/genedrpt1.htm

Voluntary System of Accountability: http://www.voluntarysystem.org/index.cfm

Resources for Further Reading

Teaching Productivity and Instructional Costs

Middaugh, M. F. "Closing In on Faculty Productivity Measures." In *Planning for Higher Education* 24, no. 2 (Winter 1996): 1–12. Ann Arbor: Society for College and University Planning, 1996.

Middaugh, M. F. "How Much Do Faculty Really Teach?" In *Planning for Higher Education* 27, no. 2 (Winter 1998): 1–12. Ann Arbor: Society for College and University Planning, 1998.

Middaugh, M. F. "Using Comparative Cost Data." In M. F. Middaugh (ed.), *Analyzing Costs in Higher Education: What Institutional Researchers Need to Know*. New Directions for Institutional Research, no. 106. San Francisco: Jossey-Bass, 2000.

Middaugh, M. F. *Understanding Faculty Productivity: Standards and Benchmarks for Colleges and Universities*. San Francisco: Jossey-Bass, 2001.

Middaugh, M. F. "A Benchmarking Approach to Managing Instructional Costs and Enhancing Faculty Productivity." *Journal for Higher Education Strategists* 1, no. 3 (Fall 2003): 221–241.

Middaugh, M. F. "Understanding Higher Education Costs." *Planning for Higher Education* 33, no. 3 (Spring 2005): 5–18.

Middaugh, M. F. "Creating a Culture of Evidence: Academic Accountability at the Institutional Level." In L. Lapovsky and D. Klinger (ed.), *Strategic Financial Challenges for Higher Education: How to Achieve Quality, Accountability, and Innovation*. New Directions for Higher Education, no. 140. San Francisco: Jossey-Bass, 2007.

Middaugh, M. F., R. Graham, and A. Shahid. *A Study of Higher Education Instructional Expenditures: The Delaware Study of Instructional Costs and Productivity* (NCES 2003-161). Washington, DC: U.S. Department of Education/National Center for Education Statistics, 2003.

Middaugh, M. F., and D. E. Hollowell. "Examining Academic and Administrative Productivity Measures." In C. S. Hollins (ed.), *Containing Costs and Improving Productivity in Higher Education*. New Directions for Institutional Research, no. 75. San Francisco: Jossey-Bass, 1992.

Effective Communication of Data and Information

Tufte, E. R. *The Visual Display of Quantitative Information*. Cheshire, CT: Graphics Press, 1983.

Tufte, E. R. *Envisioning Information*. Cheshire, CT: Graphics Press, 1990.

Tufte, E. R. *Visual Explanations: Images and Quantities, Evidence and Narrative*. Cheshire, CT: Graphics Press, 1997.

INDEX

Page references followed by *fig* indicate illustrated figures; followed by *e* indicate exhibits; followed by *t* indicate tables.